With
Flaming
Zeal

A native of Ballymena, Northern Ireland, Lionel Fitzsimons became conscious of a missionary calling soon after becoming a Christian. Formerly a civil servant, he trained at what is now Glasgow Bible College. Turned down for overseas service on medical grounds, with his wife Margaret he has been involved for thirty years in outreach to ethnic Asians in England, first in London, then in Bradford, where they still live. They are members of the missionary society, SIM, and of Sunbridge Road Mission Church.

Lionel has written several published articles on missionary priorities, and one book, 'Not At Home - British Muslims and the Gospel'. He is convinced of the need for long term commitment to missionary work - hence this new book.

With Flaming Zeal

LIONEL FITZSIMONS

AMBASSADOR

BELFAST ◆ **GREENVILLE**
NORTHERN IRELAND **SOUTH CAROLINA**

ISBN 1 84030 019 1

Ambassador Publications
a division of
Ambassador Productions Ltd.
Providence House
16 Hillview Avenue,
Belfast, BT5 6JR
Northern Ireland

Emerald House
1 Chick Springs Road, Suite 206
Greenville,
South Carolina 29609, USA

Contents

Preface

❖

E very generation is called by God to be involved with Him
in His World Mission. Here are eight short biographies
of ordinary men and women who obeyed God's call on
their lives and served Him in different parts of the world. Four
came from Scotland, two from England, one from Northern
Ireland and one from the USA.

There are several common threads running through these
biographies. Firstly, there is evidence of tested character that
the Lord of the harvest refined before releasing each of them for
cross-cultural mission in distant places. Proving God at home is
vital preparation for effective service abroad.

Secondly, willingness to endure hardship for the sake of Christ
is a recurring theme in these stories. Some faced physical
danger, others the ravages of disease and some the discourage-
ment of little tangible success in their mission. Endurance is a
noted quality in each of these people. In spite of the problems
they would not give up their ministry.

The third common factor is a recognition that each was far from perfect. They were people like you and me. They were just "jars of clay" which contained the treasure of Christ's living presence in them.

God still looks for these characteristics in men and women today who want to serve Him. May the reading of these biographies inspire and inform you so that you may follow in their footsteps and reach out to peoples still without a knowledge of Jesus Christ, the only Saviour.

Stanley Davies
General Secretary
Evangelical Missionary Alliance
Whitefield House
London

Introduction

❖ ─────────────────────

Religious exclusiveness and dogmatism are deeply unfash-
ionable in the West. The idea of spending most of a life
time overseas, trying to convert people, is alien even to
some professing Christians. Why then a book on eight missionaries very much in the traditional mould? Firstly, because
they challenge our woolly and un-Biblical thinking. Secondly,
because even among those who do believe Jesus is the only
way to God, there is an increasing emphasis on short-term
missionary service. We are in danger of forgetting that it takes
time to become an effective witness to the Lord Jesus in
another culture. Even today, a large element of sacrifice, a
willingness to burn boats, is part of the missionary calling.

That commitment of a whole life takes place in an
atmosphere of obedient love, towards God and the lost world of
fellow human beings. The love of Christ made these great
missionaries go to the ends of the earth, and kept them there
too. Missionaries like these are still needed, and sometimes

even wanted - for love is the universal language. Conditions and attitudes change rapidly. Western missionaries can seldom now go as leaders, but only as helpers. They have no Empire behind them, and may be subject to severe restrictions. Yet the world's spiritual need is the same, and only the unchanging dying-to-self love of Christ will do for today and tomorrow, as for yesterday.

Harry Merriweather's life-story has never before been published. The others have little about them in print. A new generation should learn of their achievements as channels of God's grace.

This book aims to be simple and popular in approach. Scholarly researchers will find nothing original in it, unless it be some error of fact, for which apology is made in advance! However it does try to present a true picture of the missionaries as real people, "warts and all". The very fact that they were not superhuman makes all the more searching their question to us, "Who follows where we led?".

Critics of Christianity might point to the element of brain-washing in the children of godly and missionary-minded parents. They might remark on the quirks in some of the characters portrayed. But nothing can explain away their marvellous achievements. Here are people of widely different backgrounds, denominations, temperaments, held together by the conviction that because Christ died and rose again, it is possible for humans to return forgiven to God and live in communion with Him. They had all experienced, and proclaimed, spiritual rebirth. Apart from these vital beliefs, the only other common feature we can discern is their persistent energy and faith (shown long before they left their native shores).

Said John Eliot, first missionary to the native peoples of North America: "Prayer and pains, by faith in Jesus Christ, will accomplish anything". Glory to God for what He did through such as these - and may still do, through such as us.

Mary Slessor
1848 - 1915

❖

"I did not use to believe the story of Daniel in the lions' den, until I had to take some of those awful marches, and then I knew it was true. Many a time I walked along praying, 'O God of Daniel, shut their mouths', and He did. Or I would ask the bearers or paddlers to sing all the time, for ye ken what like their singing is - it would frighten any decent respectable leopard" (Livingstone, p.100).

She was pint sized and red-haired, with that force of character such people often seem to possess. And how she needed it, not only in Nigerian jungles but from earliest childhood. Daughter of an Aberdeen shoemaker, who beat his wife and six children and left barely enough from his drinking habit to keep them alive, Mary Slessor was working in jute mills at the age of eleven. It was six hours at the loom, six hours at the mill school, week in and week out. The year she started work was the year of the great Revival, 1859.

That was a significant year for overseas missions, as we saw in the lives of Gilmour and Chalmers. But the Revival also sparked off the greatest explosion of voluntary charitable work the world has ever seen, adorned with the names of Shaftesbury, Barnardo, Fegan, Muller, and Quarrier among others. All of these men took up "the childrens' cause" in one way or another. Between them they laid the basis of our Welfare State. They were convinced that children had a right to protection, love, food, clothing and education. In Mary Slessor's childhood, these ideas, so obvious to us, were not in the programme of any political party.

Mary's mother did her best to set up the new home in Dundee, where they had moved when Mary was small. The children were sent to Sunday School, and taken to church. The mother had a deep interest in the mission of the United Presbyterians on the Calabar Coast of Nigeria. When Mary played at Sunday School her imaginary pupils were always curly-headed little Africans.

In the evenings the mother would read them stories from her magazines, about the cruel heathen customs. The children were agog. Robert the elder son volunteered to go as a missionary, and this impulse his mother encouraged. However both he and a younger brother died young, just two more victims of the insanitary housing and primitive conditions of those days.

With a father who kept losing his job through drink, and a mother unfit to work much, responsibilities too heavy for a teenager fell on Mary's slim shoulders. Soon she was doing ten hours a day at the mill. When not studying a text-book or one of the classics at her loom, it was often missionary magazines she pored over.

And of all the places mentioned there, it was Calabar that kept echoing in her mind and heart. After eighty years labour there, the Scottish Missionary Society had to report that many repulsive tribal customs were still openly practiced. Mary burned to do something to stamp them out, and she intended to use only the love of Christ to do it. Although she attributed her own conversion to hearing an old woman speak of the misery of Hell, Mary might well have taken as a text for her life, "God is love". Everyone was attracted by her warm nature, and she wanted to go to the African people with a message of the crucified love of Jesus for them too.

But her father died, and it was several more years at the mill first, as mainstay of the family now, for she had no other brothers. Meantime, how could she be of service to Christ in Dundee? Mary had always been the best Bible student in her Sunday School, and now she put her knowledge to use as a teacher there. Soon she began to notice the big boys and girls who hung aimlessly around the port area, learning bad habits and getting into mischief. How pleased she was when a Christian friend started a little mission-hall in those grubby streets. She joined him as a helper and eventually had unusual success, even with the toughest.

They resented anyone trying to talk to them about changing their lives, and one evening they surrounded her threateningly, the leader swinging a piece of lead on a string near her face. Mary didn't flinch then - or ever. Her courage and persistence had its reward, for some of these youngsters came to believe in Christ for themselves. The leader of that gang, years later, sent her a photograph of himself as a grown man with wife and children, writing that what he had learned from her made a turning point in his life. She hung the photograph on the mud wall of her hut in Africa. One of her old factory mates said, "Three weeks after I met her, I became a different girl". In Mary, along with the toughness of Northern granite, went a gentle sympathetic nature trained by personal pain to speak sincerely to troubled people. Nothing was too menial for her either - she regularly scrubbed out the mission-hall.

Does all this give the impression of an earnest religious fanatic? Actually, Mary was full of fun. Even as an adult she was known as a practical joker, and her face was almost continually smiling. It was her love that made her cheerful and strong and brave.

"Mary, Mary!" shouted one of her sisters as she reached home from the factory one day in early 1874, "Have you heard the news? David Livingstone has died in Africa!" Mary, by now a mature woman of twenty-six, decided her time of bread-winning was over. God would take care of the younger ones, now left school, and the mother. She must apply to go to Nigeria. She wrote off, was accepted, and burst into tears. The long years of waiting were ended. As her biographer W. P. Livingstone puts it, "The Dundee weaving girl was now going to one of the wildest parts of Africa, to weave there the lives of the people into new and beautiful patterns".

She sailed in 1876 and enjoyed the journey to Africa with all its exotic sights and sounds, none more so than the banks of the Calabar River, with its crocodiles, parrots and monkeys, and all the water birds, pink and white among the mangroves and palm trees along the shore line. Although the area of Calabar Town itself was far from attractive, her first few weeks were comparatively idyllic, with sympathetic senior missionaries, lots of children to play with, and only the language to begin. Later she was taken into the bush and saw things as they really were.

At that time the slave trade flourished, and indeed only the chiefs and richest tribal members were free men - the common people usually belonged to someone else and were cruelly treated by their masters. Drunken orgies and fighting seemed to be a regular occurrence, with murder and cannibalism as a result. The people feared evil spirits and sacrificed to them. When a chief died, all his wives and slaves were killed and buried with his body.

"What are those pots?" asked Mary of a native friend as they tramped through the jungle. "Oh, they are used for twin babies, Ma". "You mean, to wash them?" "No, no, Ma. The babies are killed because they are a bad omen. Or they are squeezed into these pots and left out in the forest for the wild animals. The mother is sent away too, because it is her fault that twins were born". Mary burned to stop such customs, but had to wait quietly, learning the language, which she did quickly and well. Later she taught for a time in the mission school.

After three years she caught fever very badly, and was sent back to Scotland for an early furlough. At this point she was still very shy, and could hardly be prevailed upon to speak in public about her work except to children. But she must have impressed, for on her return she was put in charge of Old Town. Maybe it was her habit of wearing old clothes and eating the same food as themselves that made the Africans confide in her. At any rate, she soon found out that the inland people were being kept from trading in the town by threats and pickets on the main paths. She stopped that simply by allowing the bush traders to enter the market through her garden.

Her first real campaign however was in rescuing two babies. At last the Government and tribal authorities were shamed into forbidding the practice of killing twins, but it still went on in secret. She told the story of Jesus in the worst parts of the town and out in the villages. In fact, she was always wanting to reach villages and tribes further afield, and her life was spent in visiting and surveying different areas that people brought to her attention. Already she was gaining a reputation as an arbitrator and pleader on behalf of suffering people, and even the heathen chiefs had a healthy respect for her stubbornness and quick tongue.

Her second home leave was taken because she was so worn out by catching a particularly virulent fever in a storm. Tornadoes were common in the area, and just before she returned to Scotland another one had demolished her mud house. She arrived back in Dundee with a baby girl she had rescued, and had her baptized as "Janie", after her youngest and last remaining sister.

During her deputation tour she had one remarkable meeting at a Bible Class in Falkirk. No fewer than six of the girls later went as missionaries to Calabar! Mary Slessor truly had the magnetism of a big heart given in an even bigger cause. However, her love of Calabar was not allowed to make her neglectful of her own family. She settled her ageing mother and the sister at a cottage in Devon, before returning to Africa, to another station, Creek Town. Now she lived even more frugally than before, sending part of her small allowance to pay for the cottage in England. Soon that need ended, as both mother and sister died. The grief went very deep; now she was alone in the world. She could comfort herself with her mother's words, "You are my child, given to me by God, and I have given you back to Him. When He needs you and where He sends you, there I would have you be."

In her hour of human desolation, there were the beloved African orphans, who were brought up one by one, the eldest helping the youngest. Apart from her adopted children, there were always temporary waifs and strays filling her little house. She was a marvel of energy and concern, dispensing medicines, teaching a church, caring for a large family and visitors. Busy, and satisfied - in a way.

Yet always the bush beyond called to her, and she set off on the first of many pioneering trips in the unexplored hinterland of Nigeria. The first area she stayed in for some time was called Okoyong. The people, says Livingstone, were "strong, proud, warlike, and had been the terror of the whole country. Every man, woman and child of them went about armed... They roamed about in bands watching the forest paths, and attacked and captured all they met, and sold them as slaves or sent them away to be food for the cannibals. They and the people of the coast were sworn enemies". No wonder it was felt advisable to first ask them whether they wanted a missionary! They said "No" for a whole year. Then Mary (or Ma, as she was usually called by now) took things into her own hands, and borrowed a state canoe from the Christian king of Creek Town, Eyo.

Arriving at Okoyong, she was surprised to find a welcome - her name and perhaps her reputation had travelled ahead, and anyway the love just shone from her face. After looking around, she returned to Creek Town to prepare for a move to Okoyong. Naturally, all the adopted children went with her!

The savage people may have accepted the idea of her coming, but were unwilling to help her in any way. She set up house in a little broken-down shack, watching with horror the constant dancing, drinking and blood-sacrifices that went on all around. Among the slave women few wanted to be her friend - they feared the white woman even more than they did their masters. Only one woman, the sister of the king, befriended the missionary. This person, Eme Ete, was indeed a faithful helper to "Ma", and attended most of her meetings; but her love for Mary Slessor never became love for Mary's Saviour, and she died a heathen.

Mary's approach was through the children first. She started a school, and some of the adults gathered around too, learning not only the principles of education, but the principles of the Gospel too. This they were quite happy to do - it was only when the Gospel and its little advocate challenged their evil customs, that they reacted. Mary decided to intervene in one of the trials by ordeal that passed for justice there. A man had been accused of witchcraft, and condemned to death. Mary, knowing he was innocent, stood between him and the chief's execution party. There followed another more deadly confrontation on the lines of the one in Dundee with the gang leader. Again Mary Slessor's steadfast fearless persuasiveness won the day. The man's sentence was commuted to a severe flogging.

The next episodes in Ma's diplomatic career were even more amazing. Hearing that a neighbouring king was dying, and that his wives and slaves would be killed to accompany him into the great Unknown, she rushed off to his village and nursed him back to health. Scarcely had she returned when the chief of her own village, convinced by a witchdoctor that some persons had made *him* fall ill, condemned them to die. Mary's fervent prayer resulted in his being brought back to health, and only one woman was killed. Next came the visit of a drunken violent group from another village, and the stirring up of antagonism between them and their hosts. Ma headed off a clash, and then led the drunk men away from another village they decided to attack. Even tually the sparks of tribal warfare died out, through God's answer to her prayers and pleadings.

After putting up a new improved mud and wattle house with her own hands, she set to the task of building a place of worship, with the help of the friendly chief and others. Before it was officially opened she insisted that people who attended should be "decently" dressed. That meant making clothes, or getting them sent from Scotland! Although many of the men never attended, the Gospel of Calvary love (like the leaven it is compared to in the Bible) was getting into the whole of tribal society. After some time Mary saw that the people wouldn't drink or fight so much if they could trade with the Calabar Coast. Naturally the chiefs laughed at this notion. Trade with their long-time enemies? How could that ever be? Mary had the answer. She took a party of chiefs (unarmed) downriver to Calabar, and they arranged a trade pact with King Eyo Honesty.

No wonder the woman's reputation spread far and wide, reaching the ears of the British colonial government. Her influence was nothing short of astounding. She prevailed not only against the tribespeople's distrust of a white female, but against their attachment to their own customs, and fear of breaking them.

It was a terrible struggle to persuade the king, when his son died, to let the occasion pass without any human sacrifice. This breakthrough came only after days and nights of watchfulness, prayer and persuasion. Most of the sacrifices and trials by ordeal (drinking poisoned water) were done to the accompaniment of much palm wine, and when sober again the tribesmen saw their own foolishness. Or perhaps they were being influenced by a different Spirit.

The chief of her own village came to her and said, "Go on, Ma, and teach us to do away with the bad old customs. We are weary of them, they bind us like chains, and we need you to help us". Several times she stopped a fight between two villages simply by the authority of her presence. For she had a regal dignity, mixed with humility, which appealed to all kinds of people, and made them respect and love her as not many others have been respected and loved.

It is no surprise that she collapsed and had to go home to Scotland for over a year. She had always lived as near native style as possible, and this in a region known as "the white man's grave". A furlough in her homeland re-invigorated her, and also introduced her children to the loyal band of supporters of all ages. She returned to widen her power and influence still more. Eme Ete her motherly native friend was her instant source of information when trouble was brewing. Ma would be off at a run to pour oil on troubled waters again, and deliver her considered opinion, which was more and more accepted as binding. She used all possible means to uncover secret wrong-doing, for by now no tribe or group could openly announce a raid or reprisal. Usually she got wind of it in time.

Presently she was appointed Vice-Consul, and wore a blue and gold cap (similar to the one which appears in some photographs of David Livingstone). No chief ever exercised such power as the White Queen of Okoyong did - and hers was totally without force! On one occasion however, when the tribespeople proved rather naughty by hiding an intended victim, she called for the British Consul-General himself. He arrived to find her mending a roof, but was soon seated with the chiefs giving them a firm official warning, which helped further to stop the killings at funerals, and the murder of twin babies.

This last custom was a real heartbreak to Ma from her earliest days, when she was shown babies in the bush who had been squashed into a waterpot and left for the wild animals. Quite often her loving attention was too late. Then she would grieve deeply. The ones who did recover she placed with Christian families, or raised herself. Her large, changing family of adopted babies meant constantly being awakened at night. Resourceful as ever, she rigged up a string to each hammock, and tied the other ends to her own bed. When a baby woke and cried, she would rock it to sleep again without having to get up! But dawn must often have found her comforting the sick and dying ones. She gave her all to them, as to everyone.

The children as they grew up loved her and wanted to help, and some became very expert baby-minders. Their help was certainly needed, for according to one biographer, Ma nursed several hundred twins in her lifetime, mainly in a little two-roomed hut. Many of the abandoned children died from exposure or ill-treatment before she reached them, but her prompt response to need, scathing words, and bitter grief when the babies died, were affecting the people's attitudes slowly but surely. In her lifetime this and other evil customs had virtually died out.

David Livingstone's rather notorious remark about going to open up a path for commerce and Christianity could equally well apply to Mary Slessor. She was always encouraging the natives to trade and increase their possessions, and regarded missionaries as the best Empire-builders. In this assumption of Western and white supremacy she was merely a child of her age. Like most missionaries she believed the British Empire could best be extended by consulting the highest interests of the subject peoples. She was no exploiter - our story so far rules that out firmly, and her exhausting labours to better the lot of her people went on and on.

Smallpox came, and many died, Mary nursing them night and day. Her friend the chief died in the middle of the night, deserted by all his followers for fear of contracting the disease. Mary immediately hammered together a coffin, dug a grave, and buried him herself. Fever laid her low, and she was finally persuaded to take a holiday in Scotland to preserve her life. She took the four children with her, and spent some months in the South of England and in the Edinburgh district of Joppa. Then when the fever had subsided, she began a deputation tour on behalf of the Mission.

Just before this furlough one of the few strange and foolish things associated with Mary Slessor occurred. She accepted a proposal of marriage from Charles Morrison, a new worker of the Calabar Mission. She cannot have been firmly convinced their engagement was God's will, for when the Mission Council decided he should remain in Duke Town rather than join her in Okoyong, she accepted it with few qualms. In the event, Mr. Morrison soon had to return to Scotland through ill-health.

In deputation meetings the essential paradox of the woman appeared most obvious. She who had outfaced drunken warriors and on one occasion had beaten off an angry hippopotamus, was trembling at her public engagements; though she spoke clearly and well once she lost herself in pleading for more missionaries. "O Britain, surfeited with privilege! Tired of Sabbath and Church; would that you would send over to us what you are throwing away!" Ma Slessor was sold out for God, and cut short her furlough to return to the Okoyong Creek.

The next three years were some of the most trying of her life, full of illness, endless consultations with native chiefs, and still doing her own repairs and building, as well as the care of all the churches. At least Ma now had two women missionaries nearby, who were attentive to her needs; but no-one could stop her pushing her poor body to its absolute limits. Always there was the tension between the ongoing work and the vision of advance into virgin teritory. No duty was allowed to be neglected, but the strain of being everything to everyone pulled the great little woman down, and she decided to resign her vice-consulship for good. However later, as we shall see, she was appointed chair of a native court in Enyong District. Livingstone quotes a government official of that time. "I have seen her get up and box the ears of a chief because he continued to interrupt after being warned to be quiet. The act caused the greatest amusement to the other chiefs".

In one of her times of recovering vitality she laid the foundations of a new settlement at Use, for women and girls. Then as soon as she was assured it would be developed and staffed by others, it became her greatest preoccupation to move on.

This time it was to the Enyong Creek, north-west of the main Calabar River. At that time a fierce tribe, the Aros, dealt in slaves obtained by raiding other villages. They had particularly horrible jujus (idols that cast a spell) and priests who encouraged them in the profitable occupation of slave-catching and thereby defying the British Government. Eventually an expeditionary force was sent to quell them, and did so at the cost of many Aro lives. The adventure of moving into the subdued tribe was a new challenge to Mary's devotion and zeal. She adopted the approach already proved successful at Okoyong, by opening a school first, then some time later a church.

On her other station, Akpap in Okoyong district, she was now joined by a Miss Wright, her first and only helper and companion. They made a well-suited pair; Ann Wright was a teacher and loved children too. Her presence made it easier for Ma to visit the two African girls she had stationed at Itu among the Aros. All her first group of adopted girls were now growing up, and each had a job to do. Most of the family had received Christ as Saviour and Lord, due largely to the family prayers held each day by Ma. This she always made time for, however busy she was. Her love and prayers were producing young evangelists among destitute children, and they took over some of the work she established. This left her free to answer the call of the great unreached Beyond.

But she was only one woman, however greatly devoted. In each of her furloughs in Britain she pleaded for helpers to buy up the opportunities in Iboland. Until near the end of her life, sadly, no-one was willing to come out of the coastal stations into the even more primitive hinterland, where she struggled on, an indomitable romantic figure burning out her strength for God through the people. The physical difficulties of sleeping in the open-air, eating native food and drinking unfiltered water, being caught in torrential downpours and laid low with recurring fevers, would have killed or driven home most strong men. She was able to accept them, not grudgingly but joyfully. Even loneliness Mary joked over in her letters home. "I have been here seven weeks without one scrap from the outside; letter or paper - nothing to read but the old advertisement sheets of papers lining the press and the boxes. If you wish for the names of hotels or boarding houses in any part of Europe - send to me. I have them all at my tongue's end".

Finally people did begin to come from Scotland to take over the various stations she had pioneered alone, and she was free to go off again. Roads of a sort were being built inland now, and one of her friends among the British officers bought her a bicycle. Overcoming her first idea that it was an "infernal machine", and herself too old to ride it, she soon became a familiar figure on the new routes between villages, saving at least some of her energy. A small hospital, the Mary Slessor Mission Hospital, was built, but she never worked in it. She was much more at home exploring the rivers and creeks, seeking the redemption, in Jesus' Name, of the native tribes.

Actually, her greatest hindrance in this work had become her own reputation. Constantly she was being called upon to arbitrate and advise. not only by the Africans but also by the British officials, with whom she was extremely popular. After a time of freedom, she was given the job of vice-president of the Native Court, giving her the powers of a judge. Her 'case-law' was her wide knowledge of native customs and practices.

A return to Scotland was now long overdue, but before going she took on one last job - supervising the building of a rest-home for missionaries in Calabar! Only then did she allow herself a holiday. This time she took only the youngest boy, Daniel, who was a great favourite with everyone. So much so, that he did not wish to return to Africa! Mary however was soon restless. Her beloved Scotland was no longer home to her, and Africa called her back - to die. Although no-one who met her then knew she would never return to them, the final meetings were full of poignancy and power.

Soon it was as if she had never been away; days full of teaching, adjudicating and explaining, as well as looking after her friends and other more menial tasks. W.P. Livingstone says she often preached in ten to twelve villages in one Sunday! Such a work-load on such a poor frail body. She was almost constantly ill now, but nothing kept her from the work. Even though many younger missionaries lived nearby and helped her (one from that meeting in Falkirk), her years of unremitting toil and iron self-discipline would not allow her to rest or be ministered to for long. Apart from a few visits to Calabar, she never took any time off, until forced to by really serious illness. It took a long time to recover, and Mary used the time to think out her most ambitious plan, to open a home and school for orphan girls and train them up to responsible womanhood. As always, Mary's dreams were those of a very practical person, and although she herself was never able to do it, the vision was later taken up by others and brought to fruition.

It was no wonder that other tribes were constantly asking her to set up churches and live amongst them. They recognised in her all that was best in the white man's culture, infused and transformed by her deep love of God and the people. Somewhere beneath all the desire for material advancement (which Mary herself never criticised in them) was a longing to be free from all the old fears and cruelties. Ma Slessor was able by her remarkable personal influence to keep the colonial government of Iboland based on Christian principles, fair and just. But far more than that is her achievement. By the power of the Holy Spirit, men and women and children were turned into real Christians, with the holy life of Christ beating within them. Not personality, but much prayer, sacrifice and patient love availed her there.

Finally the strain of opening another new station at Ikpe, and at the same time carrying on the existing work at Use, laid her low. Even then she wouldn't have given in unless ordered to by a young mission doctor whom she respected and loved. Just as before, the simple affection of a child restored her. In fact, many children wrote to her from Scotland. She delighted in replying in her own playful and enthusiastic way. Once she had recovered enough to travel, another Scottish supporter paid for her to have a real break in the Canary Islands. She was overwhelmed by the love shown to her there, but of course her own ministry to others flowed on, and one little crippled boy met there, wrote to her for years afterwards and received inspiration and courage from her great resources. Imagine a person who in the midst of great responsibilities could take time to write of the birds, animals and flowers of Nigeria in such a way as to fire the imagination of a boy. That was Mary Slessor.

Such a life, humble and retiring as it was, could not for ever escape wider notice. As her Lord had said, a city set on a hill cannot be hidden, and soon Mary was amazed to hear that she had been awarded the Cross of St. John of Jerusalem (still a coveted honour). For Mary it was particularly fitting that the British Empire should honour her. She had a faith (perhaps naive, perhaps not) that Britons could, by their ingenuity and persistence, make the world a better place, given a chance! She probably never dreamed that black people are capable of just as much as whites. But there was nothing of the bigot in Mary. She was prepared to give her African friends equal treatment - her whole life is singularly free of anything patronizing. Also, she was the eternal optimist.

It is almost unbelievable (for us who know so little of what God can do with an obedient person) that Mary, exhausted as she was, found time and energy to open and run a third station. To Ikpe and Use, she added Odoro, and shuttled between the three, establishing a new church and confirming the two already in existence. "She was a wreck, her body was a mass of pain, she was growing deaf and blind and oh, so lonely! Yet her heart was bursting with love and gratitude and joy. O wonderful Ma!" So says her first biographer, and we can only echo his words. Add to this catalogue the fact that at that time she often couldn't obtain enough food, and we see a woman who like the Apostle Paul was constrained, pressed in by one thing only. Writing to a little friend her words speak volumes. "Are you going to do some-thing fine in the New Year? I trust so. At least you will be good, and TO BE is a better verb than TO DO, in my estimation".

The outbreak of World War in 1914 was a bitter blow to her. She fell into a terrible fever, and died on January 13th, 1915, after an illness of five months.

For about forty years she had toiled, wept and prayed with no thought of reward, except of knowing that she did God's will. The great recognition that now began would have embarrassed her intensely; but it was only a small thing compared to the praise she will be accorded by the Lamb in the midst of the Throne of Heaven.

"Write: Blessed are the dead who die in the Lord from now on. 'Yes', says the Spirit, 'they will rest from their labour, for their deeds will follow them'".   Revelation, 14: 13.

James Gilmour

1843 - 1891

❖

James Gilmour died of typhus in the large city of Tientsin, China, far from the grassy wastes of his mission-field. Yet when other missionaries visited Mongolia, some time after his death, they were met with eager questions from people as to why their old friend had not accompanied them. "When the Christians heard the sad news, grown-up men burst into tears and sobbed like children; while many who had never bowed the knee to Gilmour's Master, lamented loudly that they would never again see a man they regarded as so good and noble".

This man, in the opinion of one of his colleagues, endured as much physical discomfort and loneliness for the Gospel as the Apostle Paul himself. James Gilmour was born in June 1843 at Cathkin, a village in Lanarkshire. Cathkin Braes are today a Strathclyde landmark, just inside the Glasgow City boundary. In those days the area was quite rural. Gilmour's father was the village wheelwright, a self-employed craftsman more prosperous than most working-class people. Puritan values of thrift and industry ruled the home and six children. The parents were loyal members of Dr. Ralph Wardlaw's congregation in Glasgow, and used to walk the five miles each way to Sunday worship. All the children went with them from an early age.

James Gilmour grew up on the whole a very balanced individual, but, as we shall see later, extreme in one or two minor matters. He was an extremely strong-minded boy, who usually preferred his own company on his roamings to collect geological specimens. Very studious, he was surprisingly full of fun and love of adventure. As a young man, he part sailed, part dragged a little boat up the Clyde to Hamilton. The trip was arduous if not dangerous - a foretaste of his later life.

His parents encouraged his studies, and he easily won a scholarship to Glasgow University. John Paterson, his best friend there, remarked, "There was not a shred of indolence in his nature; it may be truthfully said that he never wilfully lost an hour". His efforts after scholarly distinction were at this stage motivated partly by pride. His heart was not yet given to Christ; he was not yet born again. That great change took place in the middle of his M.A. course, and he then began to look on his studies as the first step in becoming a minister of the Gospel.

Although he had a natural flair for languages, his fellow-students were very surprised when towards the end of his course he announced that he would go overseas as a missionary. As he won prize after prize, this promising young man had given every indication of being cut out for academic life, or perhaps to be the minister of a fashionable parish. What caused his amazing decision to go overseas? The reasoning comes out in a famous quotation, given at length because of its wider importance:

"Having decided as to the capacity in which I should labour in Christ's Kingdom (that is, as a minister), the next thing which occupied my serious attention was the locality where I should labour. Occasionally before I had thought of the relative claims of the home and foreign fields, but during the summer season I thought the matter out, and decided for the mission field; even on the low ground of common sense I seemed called to be a missionary.

"Is the Kingdom a harvest-field? Then I thought it reasonable that I should go where the work was most abundant, and the workers fewest. Labourers say they are overtaxed at home: what then must be the case abroad, where there are wide stretching plains already white to harvest, with scarcely here and there a solitary reaper...?

"But I go out as a missionary, not that I may obey the dictates of common sense, but that I may obey that command of Christ, 'Go into all the world, and preach...'. He Who said 'Preach', said also 'Go ye into', and what Christ has joined together, let no man put asunder.

"This command seems to me to be strictly a missionary injunction, and as far as I can see, those to whom it was first delivered saw it in that light. So that, apart altogether from choice or other lower reasons, my going forth is a matter of obedience to a plain command; and in place of seeking to assign a reason for going abroad, I would prefer to say that I have failed to discover any reason why I should stay at home".

He applied to the London Missionary Society, and was accepted for theological training at the Congregational Union college in Cheshunt, Herts, for two years. Later he did a one year missionary course, and again graduated with honours. During that last year he made the acquaintance of a Mrs. Swan, widow of one of the original pioneers in Mongolia. She invited him to spend part of the vacation at her home in Edinburgh, and his heart was aroused by the needs of the great steppes of Southern Siberia. He had found his mission-field.

Not yet twenty-seven, he sailed in the early Spring of 1870 for Peking. It was a four month journey, and he spent it talking to the sailors about his Lord, and holding services for the few other passengers. It was hardly a comfortable time to arrive. The neighbouring city of Tientsin had just witnessed an anti-Westerner riot, and the killing of more than ninety people, some of them European. Several churches had also been destroyed. The violence never actually erupted in Peking, but for a time it seemed to be spreading. Gilmour and his friends prayed incessantly that God would stay the hands of evil men. What a challenge to his faith it must have been, to believe that he had not been brought all the way to China, only to be murdered!

The day rumoured for a mass assassination of "foreign devils" came; and passed quietly because it poured with rain for twenty hours without a break! Later the blood-thirst died away, but Gilmour wondered whether it might hinder the journey to Mongolia if he delayed. So he set off in a Russian camel train for the journey of more than one thousand miles, understanding very little Chinese, only a few sentences in Mongolian, and no Russian at all!

Mongolia is a vast area, which can be divided geographically into three parts. First there is Chinese Mongolia, just beyond the Great Wall, then the Gobi Desert, and further North-West again is Siberian Mongolia, then Russian, now semi-independent. Chinese Mongolia is roughly agricultural, the Gobi is desolate sand, very sparsely populated, while the plateaux of Siberian Mongolia support some grass, and therefore wandering herdsmen.

This last area was to be Gilmour's parish for some years, and the return to Tientsin, which he made very occasionally, was in itself a tremendous journey. This first one, in the opposite direction, was especially trying. It occupied fifty-four days, and included the negotiating of some very high, cold mountain passes, the crossing of dreary, hot dusty plains of desert, and one occasion when he was buried under his own baggage!

Add to these the difficulty of communicating with his fellow-travellers, the strange and unpalatable food, and above all the lack of any spiritual companionship, and it is not surprising Gilmour suffered from loneliness and depression. It was as if God was showing His servant what to expect, and nerving his spirit for the years ahead.

Neither the Russian nor the Mongolian authorities were satisfied with his papers, and he had to get new ones sent from Peking before beginning work. His first language teacher was very incompetent, if not downright mischievous. He taught

Gilmour a phrase meaning, "I am well versed in Mongolian", but told him it meant, "Excuse me, I don't know much Mongolian". It must have taken all Gilmour's natural humour to see the funny side of that!

Prompt and decisive as ever, he decided to live among the Mongolians and learn the language not from books, but by soaking himself in it. His teacher this time was a lama, a priest of the debased form of Buddhism that ruled the Mongolians' spirits. The tent where Gilmour lodged, was poor. By a rather amusing coincidence, the staple food at one stage of its preparation closely resembled porridge, and Gilmour preferred to fish it out of the pot at this stage, naming it "Scotland". It proved possible for him to pick up much of the language by listening to household conversations and taking notes, and this was interspersed with occasional lessons in a very classical high-flown form of the language, from the lama. Gilmour soon realized that most of this was quite useless to him, and to avoid arguments would suddenly rise up and go for a long walk!

Life in the tents was not always peaceful, what with family quarrels and drawn knives, the occasional fire in the roof, and so on. But after a few months, he had a fair knowledge of simple Buriat Mongol, and set off for a station occupied some forty years before by the L.M.S. pioneers, at Selenginsk, today Novoselenginsk. He found, to his surprise and joy, that a few converts from those days were alive and standing firm in faith. One had corresponded with Mrs. Swan, and was expecting him.

The tribespeople of Central Asia spent much of their time in the saddle, and just could not understand a man who had never learned to ride horse or camel. Gilmour learned the hard way in this as in most things, by riding a horse all the way back across the Gobi Desert to Kalgan on the Great Wall. Kalgan was a staging post for Mongolian and Russian traders entering the Middle Kingdom (as Chinese people called their country). He was again among missionaries, and spent a few months brushing up his knowledge of written Mongolian and talking to the camel drivers about the Lord Jesus Christ.

He then took another trip to Northern Mongolia, living in tents through the winter, and by the time of his first return to Peking in November 1871, was quite competent in the language and culture of his adopted people.

In a report he made on the advantages and disadvantages of work in the grasslands of Outer Mongolia, he listed among the disadvantages;

a) that the Mongols were afraid of any foreigner dying on their hands and causing them trouble with the authorities,

b) that chiefs were not always friendly, and

c) that "personal inconveniences" could arise, such as trouble with drunken Mongols "who are apt to draw their great knives", sickness beyond the reach of help, and exposure in wet weather when no fire could be obtained. Very typically, he set against these, three remedies: "The first of these difficulties can be got over by having two missionaries in the place of one; the second by presents, conciliatory conduct, and by not staying too long in one place; the third by faith in God, Who numbers the hairs of the heads of His servants".

So right at the beginning of his ministry he saw the essential need of a companion. Yet apart from his nearly eleven years of marriage, he laboured almost alone throughout his years in Mongolia. No male companion was able to stay more than a few weeks with him till recalled by various circumstances. He bore the loneliness heroically, and for all that was accomplished, the credit under God is his alone. He reminded the London Missionary Society that it was men, not methods, that drew other people to Christ. But no man was able to join him in being a "living letter" from Christ, known and read by the Mongolian people.

However, he did have advantages. His predecessors had left a great legacy; the Bible in the main language of Buriat, with several good tracts translated also.

Having passed one miserable winter in tents, he decided it was impossible to travel through the grasslands from caravan to caravan in the coldest weather, and so decided to make his evangelistic trips in summer. But in 1872 he went to Peking for the hot season, and learned elementary medicine from a Dr. Dudgeon. The following winter he lodged at a Buddhist temple in the city, meeting many acquaintances from the steppelands.

Now comes an episode which reveals most clearly the great decisiveness, individuality, and yet prayerful trustfulness of the man. Hearing a young lady well spoken of by her brother-in-law (a fellow missionary), he asked to be allowed to see her letters, and discovering in her one who shared his own devotion to Christ's Kingdom, proposed to and was accepted by Emily Prankard without having met or seen her (except in one of the old sepia photographs of those days). Actually, she was a pretty woman, but not strong. She arrived in November 1874, and Gilmour trekked from Mongolia out to Peking to meet the steamer. An early biographer says he wore "a rusty overcoat which had seen much service on Mongolian plains, as at that period he had not adopted Chinese dress. Round his neck was wound a large woollen comforter, for it is bitterly cold on the Pei-Ho in the dawn of a November morning. Altogether, his appearance was not exactly suggestive of a bridegroom".

The young lady, who had been brought up in then select Bexleyheath, South-East London, needed all her devotion to accompany Gilmour on even one trip. In fact she twice made the journey to Selenginsk, but then decided her place was in Tientsin, where she looked after their children and became a beloved visitor and evangelist in Chinese homes. The two journeys (which took all the summer of succeeding years) were feats of endurance and heroism for a Western lady delicately reared. On one occasion they were near to being swept away in a flood. If Gilmour's own endurance impressed the Mongols, that of his wife completely won their respect and confidence. On these trips Gilmour constantly used his recently acquired knowledge of medicine to heal illness and make yet another entrance for his Gospel to the people's hearts.

On one of their trips together, Gilmour and Emily found themselves in great danger of death. He had recommended a man with double cataracts to go to Peking to the Mission hospital. The benefits of the simple operation were reversed by unhygienic conditions after the man left the hospital, and he ended up completely blind. To add to the tragedy, a rumour was spread that Gilmour and his wife were in the pay of the doctors, who were removing the corneas of people's eyes in order to sell them to rich Westerners. The couple stayed despite the danger, and gradually re-established trust among the ignorant people.

Gilmour was a strange contrast. His views on certain matters of missionary policy set him at odds with his colleagues, and he showed his great love of argument even in dealing with his Mongol friends. But only his arguments were hard. Firm, even stubborn he was, but never malicious. He was quite capable of ending a loud-voiced discussion by offering to help his antagonist in some practical way! Great too as was his vision for the Mongols, he had no objection to filling in for other missionaries on furlough, often in quite different cultures and language areas.

Gilmour had early realised that behaviour which to him was perfectly innocent, such as leaving the tent where he was staying to have a time alone with God in prayer, or writing his journal, were looked upon with great suspicion by the people. He had willingly given up these practices in order to remove any possible hindrance to his Mongolian friends listening to the Gospel. He had taken every opportunity, by personal conversation in tents or by the wayside, as well as in the Mongol quarters of Peking and Tientsin, to spread the Gospel. He had distributed many copies of the Scriptures and countless other Christian books and tracts. Now, after several years, it became painfully obvious to him that, as the Mongols' grasp of the "foreign teaching" increased, so did their determination not to accept or act on it. When in 1882 he and the family sailed to England on furlough, he could report no conversions.

But he did have a wonderful ability to bring Mongolia to vivid life, and interest Christian people in it. He wrote a book called "Among the Mongols", which was compared by one reviewer to Defoe's "Robinson Crusoe" for its ability to make the reader feel he was there on the Asian plains. As a result, many more people began praying for the Mongol mission.

On his return to China, he was asked to superintend the Peking work in the absence of a colleague. Before Mr. Meech left for England, however, Gilmour took a walking tour through the grasslands to renew former contacts. His joy was full to hear the first confession of faith from a young man called Boyinto, who was later baptized by the missionaries at Kalgan after a period of probation. Here is Gilmour's vivid account of the thrilling discovery:

"Finding (the priest) alone, I told him I had come to speak to him and my other friends about the salvation of their souls, and was pressing him to accept Christ, when a layman I also knew entered. Without waiting for me to say anything, the priest related the drift of our conversation to the layman, who, tongs in hand, was trying to make the fire blaze. Blaze it would not, and the layman, invisible to me in the dense cloud (of smoke), though only about two yards away, spoke up and said that for months he had been a scholar of Jesus, and that...whether the priest would join him or not, his mind was made up, he would trust the Saviour...

"The place was beautiful to me as the gate of Heaven, and the words of the confession of Christ from out the cloud of smoke were inspiriting to me as if they had been spoken by an angel from out of a cloud of glory".

In the midst of happy, and at last fruitful ministry, Gilmour's worst trial began. His wife fell ill and died not long after the birth of their third child, leaving him with a sore heart to act as both parents to them. This he did to the best of his ability for some months, trying at the same time to discharge his missionary duties. But even such a loving and capable father was forced to admit that neither he nor the boys were benefitting from the experience, and he decided to send the older two to be cared for and schooled in Scotland. Less than two years after this reluctant parting the sickly toddler Alec also died.

About this time, Gilmour's work was also entering a new phase. He had considered the possibility of settling in one area, rather than itinerating from place to place. After an extensive survey of Eastern Mongolia he decided to set up his solitary dwelling in a place called Ta Ch'eng Tzu. However, he was once again starting from scratch in evangelism, as no-one had been there before him with the Gospel. Several years of thankless labour ensued. Being a born wanderer, he finally had three centres instead of one, and still travelled great distances on evangelistic tours.

As an illustration of his self-denying determination to identify with the people he served, he wrote of one trip:

" I was turned out of the two respectable inns at Bull Town because I was a foot traveller, had no cart or animal, that is, and had to put up in a tramps' tavern because I came as a tramp!" and, "I had a great time in Mongolia but Oh! so cold. Some of the days spent in the markets were so very cold that my muscles seemed benumbed, and speech even was difficult. I met with some spiritual response, though, and with that I can stand cold. ...At night I used to draw a woollen thread through the blisters. In the morning I 'hirpled' (*limped*) a little, but it was soon all right. I walked, not because I had no money to ride, but to get at the Mongol who was with me".

These physical rigours, with the unfriendliness and deceitfulness of the people, sorely tried his spirit. Especially he groaned over the hold tobacco and alcohol had on the Mongols of that area. He made non-smoking and teetotalism a condition of church membership to converts, and as a result, few joined the church and fewer still were faithful to the standards he set.

His assistants (mainly Chinese) often proved unsatisfactory, and of course a multitude of other cares pressed upon him at this time. It is all the more remarkable therefore to read his letters to Scotland, to his "dear sons Jimmie and Willie".

No-one could accuse Gilmour of neglecting his work, and he must often have been exhausted, discouraged and in pain from blisters on his feet when he sat down to write to them.

But the series of letters preserved are full of loving counsel and exhortation, mixed with interesting tales of his day-to-day experience. Here are just a few extracts, taken from letters printed often with a Chinese paint-brush (when it was too cold for ink to flow in a conventional pen!):

"I am on a journey to Mongolia. I am having wet weather, which is detaining me, but is good for the crops, so I am glad. I have a young man called Yeng with me. He is a Christian, and helps me to preach. I have your photographs with me, and I take them out at the inns and look at them. I like to see your faces; I don't feel so lonely then. I often, very often, pray for you, and try to think where you are on the ship now. You should be near the Red Sea. Oh, my dear boys, it was so hard to leave you, and I often cry yet when I think of you! I pray to Jesus to make you happy. I hope you'll grow up good and useful men. If you are earnest Christians, I think it would be nice if you became missionary doctors, and came out to heal the people's diseases just as Mama did, and tell them about Jesus. Don't you think so?"

"....I have no watch with me. The Chinese trouble me so that I think it best to leave it at home. It was so nice when in an inn at Pa Kow to hear a clock striking in a shop in the yard. I passed, one day, a very strange mountain which had been split in two. Its name in Chinese means Split Mountain.

" I met three lamas going to a far-off place to worship. Every two or three steps they lay down flat on the ground, then got up and walked another two or three steps, then prostrated themselves again. They do not know about Jesus saving people, and thought they would save themselves in this way. Poor people! Yet they don't like to hear about Jesus saving the people. They want the credit of thus saving themselves. The elm trees are just ripe now. They are the size of small fish-scales; when the wind blows they come down like snow."

"...All July I was poorly, had some fever, could not eat much, but was able to go on with my mission work as usual. There were two great fairs here, and I was anxious not to lose the opportunity, so I stuck to my work, going out to the fair with my tent. We had a great many patients, and told many people of Jesus. A good many people say the teaching and religion is good, but they are afraid to enter it. We are strange to them yet...."

"In the beginning of August we hired a cart to go to Ta Ch'eng Tzu. Thirty li from Ta Ch'eng Tzu the cart wheel broke down. They tied it up with rope. We got to an inn (four li away) and next day rode the mules to Ta Ch'eng Tzu, where a carpenter mended the wheel. At T.C.T. we had seven days and nights of rain. It was a great flood. The river rose and washed away about a hundred acres of land and forty or fifty houses..."

"Now my dear sons, may Jesus be near you and bless you much in your life and lessons. I do so hope that you will keep on praying to Jesus, and doing the things which Jesus likes, as Mama did. Don't forget your prayers, my sons..."

Gilmour's letters are a natural mixture of piety and simple story-telling. He was singularly free of the sentimentality of many Victorian Christians, but at the same time was not afraid to show his heart. As we saw, he cherished a great desire that his sons should become medical missionaries in China. This desire was doubtless born of his own experience in trying to relieve the terrible sicknesses of the people. The letters mention converts from time to time, but the great majority of these were Chinese, not Mongolians.

"We are still here. I daily go out into the street with my medicines and books and preach. Three men have said they want to be Christians, but they do not come to services, and are only half-hearted I fear. I am praying all I can for them. I pray too for you. You are very precious to me. If you do not believe in Jesus, what shall I do? I want the heathen to believe. If my own sons do not pray to Jesus, Oh, then I will be broken-hearted. But I trust you are his little disciples even now".

"There is not much more that I can tell you to interest you. The other day I was drawing a man's tooth. I got hold of it, and he shouted, 'Don't, don't - won't do, won't do!' But I pulled away steadily, and it was out in a twinkling, and the crowd roared all round with laughter. Last night again I pulled another man's tooth, pretty much with the same results. It is too lonely altogether, and it is a comfort to me to write a little to you now and again. It is like talking to you... Cheer up laddies, with your lessons; we'll see each other some day yet."

"We have had three days' wind. Eh, man, the first day the dust was terrible. But I had lots of patients, and remained out all day. At last we had to take down our tent. It could not stand. The tent was carried to the inn, but we remained with our table till evening.... The boys here buy a lot of books too, and I preach to them earnestly, because in ten years to come they will be men, and if they know about Jesus now, they may more easily become Christians soon. You Jimmie, know Jesus; does Willie? Teach him. Mama is not here to teach him, and I am far away. You are his big brother. Teach you him, like a good laddie as you are".

Probably the most affecting letter he wrote was just after the death of little Alec (or Alick as he sometimes spelled the name). The imagined dialogue between the angels and "Mama" is heavily underlined:

"Now, my dear sons, his brothers, don't be too sorry about him. He has gone to Mama and Grandma and to Jesus, in that city of beauty where no-one is ever sick and where all is beautiful. There are lots of little girls and boys playing all about, and no bad boys or bad people to annoy him or teach him evil. And would not Mama receive him with her loving arms just as she used to hold you and him when she was here. Dear dear pretty Mama, dear dear wee Alick. I think I see her hugging him, and him nestling on her bosom just when he arrived. They are for ever with the Lord. Jesus likes to see them. They like to see Jesus. The angels as they pass stop to look at them and say 'Your son?' The angels say, 'Has he any brothers or sisters?' Mama says, 'Two brothers, at school in Hamilton, Scotland'. The angels say, 'The brothers and Papa will all come one day if they belong to Jesus'".

So for five years Gilmour wrote to his boys. Only once his letters were interrupted, when he returned to Britain for a furlough and saw their progress for himself. The letters show his great joy at having a Dr. Roberts as colleague for a short time, but then Gilmour's closest friend, a Dr. Mackenzie of Tientsin, suddenly died, and Roberts was recalled to take his place. Gilmour was alone again, sick and often depressed with the difficulties of his work. When a new helper, Dr. Smith, finally arrived, his first act was to order Gilmour back to Scotland for his health's sake. This voyage was amazingly fast (six weeks), and it is probably just as well, for a long fatiguing one would probably have killed Gilmour.

His recovery though was equally speedy. After part of the summer with his boys at Millport on the Firth of Clyde, he embarked on a strenuous deputation tour, and less than eight months after arriving in the country was off again on the long return journey. During his leave, Gilmour also attended the Keswick Convention, and was deeply blessed by it. Even earlier he had become an avid reader of Bishop Handley Moule, Andrew Murray and F.B. Meyer, exponents of "the life of rest", and it was noticeable that during his later periods of service his character mellowed. He was less inclined to argue, and seemed to be quite carefree despite the frustrations of the work, and the responsibility of his family. In a letter to a missionary friend he explained:

"Before I worked, oh so hard and so much, and asked God to bless my work. Now I try to pray more and get more blessing, and then work enough to let the blessing find its way through me to men. And this is the better way..."

He reached Tientsin on March 2nd 1890, and now addressed his growing sons as, "James", and "William". Soon he had to tell them of Dr. Smith's illness and departure, and his own renewed loneliness. A new worker. Mr. Parker, did eventually join him, and noted the Christlike ministry of both preaching and healing that Gilmour maintained throughout his years of service. Many people received helpful spiritual counsel from his mature and deep Christian experience. His final letter to his sons was begun on March 16th 1891, ends with the assurance of his continuing prayers for them, and has this touching postscript, dated March 20th: "Letters come, but no news from you. Much love to you. J.G." Exactly two months later, he was dead.

So far, we have hardly noticed his relations with other missionaries. Many, both before and after his death, paid tribute to his delightfully humorous company and inspiring self-sacrifice. The one incident which caused ill-feeling in the missionary ranks around him was, if the facts be impartially sifted, far more the fault of Dr. Dudgeon than of Gilmour. It concerned only the use of a room for storing books, and its details are not worth recording. Gilmour, having in his usual argumentative way caused part of the ill-feeling, immediately did the right thing by withdrawing quietly.

James Gilmour loved his Chinese helpers and elders with a complete lack of patronizing unusual in his day among British people. It seems peculiarly fitting, therefore, to summarize the tributes to him which poured in after his death, with a last letter to his boys. It is written, not by the loving father, but by seventeen of his Chinese colleagues:

"....We who through the teaching of Pastor Gilmour have obtained the doctrine of the second birth, and received the grace of Jesus, had hoped with Mr. Gilmour to have assembled on the earth till our heads were white, and in the future life to have gone with him to Heaven. Little did we think we should have been so unhappy. He has already gone to the Lord. We certainly know he is in the presence of the Lord, not only praying for us but also for you, our brothers".

"...We pray you, when you see this letter, not to grieve beyond measure. We hope you will study with increased ardour, so as to obtain the heavenly wisdom, like Solomon, and that afterwards you may come to China to (the town of) Cha'o Yang, to preach the Gospel widely. As the father did may the sons follow, is our earnest desire.

Signed by the Cha'o Yang Christians..."

James Chalmers
1841 - 1901

❖

For sheer romance and adventure, the life of James Chalmers makes most fiction seem tame. It is amazing that one man could have experienced the dangers he did, lived so long and accomplished so much. He is a male Mary Slessor in his always pushing on to new challenges in the Lord's service. Like her, he was intensely practical, and laboured much for the betterment of his people. He believed that true civilization came to savage people only when their hearts and minds were renewed by the Holy Spirit. Such was the power of love and nobility in his personality that he came to exercise an unusual influence over the Pacific Islanders and later the Papuans.

Chalmers was born in Ardrishaig, Argyll, on that great arm of the Atlantic called Loch Fyne. He did not grow up in the same little town, because his father was a stone-mason and road-mender who from time to time was given different stretches of road to keep in repair. He was an Aberdonian, strong, silent and devout. The mother on the other hand, equally devout, was from Luss on the Loch Lomond side. She had more of the Celtic temperament; energetic, warm-hearted, talkative.

James must have been a handful. When the father returned wearily from a week on some isolated job, he would often be called upon to punish the boy who was always in a scrape. Leader in all mischief and fighting, James was three times rescued from drowning. After he became a strong swimmer, he rescued one boy who had fallen into a swollen river, one child who had fallen off the pier at Inverary, and two fellow students who had got into difficuties in the River Lea near London. In his later missionary life, he was three times more rescued from the sea; confirming his father's ironic remark that he was meant to die some other way!

Somewhere beneath all the turbulent energy and hatred of restriction there was a sensitivity and uprightness. No boy was more honest and true to his friends, nor less resented being disciplined. Maybe that element in his character is what attracted him to Gilbert Meikle, the new United Presbyterian minister at Inverary. Chalmers went to the Sunday School and Bible Class there, and continued even when he started at the Grammar School at thirteen, and then went into employment as a surveyor's assistant and later as an articled clerk to solicitors in the little burgh.

One day, in the Bible Class, Mr. Meikle read a missionary letter from a magazine. It told how the cannibals of Fiji were responding to the Gospel and being changed into Christians. Chalmers was enthralled. Mr. Meikle closed the lesson by asking, "Is there perhaps some boy here who will one day be a missionary and bring the Gospel to the cannibals in other islands?". Chalmers said nothing, but on the way home he had the impulse to jump over a wall, crouch down, and pray that God might send him.

At the same time he was still leading a gang of rather rough teenagers who wasted their time hatching up wild schemes of mischief. One early summer's morning, he and two others crept down to the harbour intending to "borrow" a rowing-boat, go to

Greenock and join up as seamen. At the last moment Chalmers had a vision of his mother's grief when she discovered his going. He turned back.

Chalmers was eighteen in 1859, the year of the great Ulster Revival. Two evangelists from the North of Ireland stopped off at Inverary. On Mr. Meikle's invitation, they held some meetings at his church. "Going along this evening?", called out James Chalmers' friend, old Mr. McNicol. "Well, I...maybe", replied Chalmers. He did go, and was overpowered by their earnestness and the unction of the Holy Spirit on their preaching of the Cross. Off he stumbled to think and pray about his sinfulness. Then he sought out Mr. Meikle, who led him to faith in Christ. He handed over his wild self-will to Jesus as Saviour and Lord, and his energy was now directed to Sunday School teaching and lay-preaching.

It was not long before he thought of that earlier vow to become a missionary. True, it had been made when he was not yet born again; but he felt it still binding on him. Yet how could he go to university and become a minister or doctor? He had no great love for advanced study. Neither could his parents afford to support him. Eventually Mr. Meikle arranged for him to join the Glasgow City Mission, and at the same time to do some study at the University there. He cannot have had time for much reading, for his work among the poor people in the closes around the High Street was demanding. He later said that, apart from cannibalism, he saw worse things done in Glasgow than in Papua or Rarotonga. However, after eight months he was accepted for training at the Cheshunt College of the Congregational Churches.

Again he found study a burden, but pressed on and finished the course creditably. Apart from the episode of rescuing his fellow students from drowning, he was popular for his good humour and preaching ability. One evening he dressed in a bear-skin and crept into the dining-hall, growling fiercely. Everyone scattered, and Chalmers just managed to get his teeth into someone's trousers while an accomplice blew out the light. When it was lit again, Chalmers was revealed laughing heartily with the bear-skin still over his shoulders. From being a thin wiry lad, he was developing the magnificent physique which was to bear him through many difficult situations and keep him free of serious illness throughout his life.

He often used to paddle an old canoe on the Lea, and this skill stood him in good stead later, among the breakers of the South Seas. He was also in charge of a church extension project at Hertford Heath, and would walk the eight miles each way in all weathers. His ministry was greatly appreciated by the little group who worshipped there. For a third year of training he went on to the London Missionary Society's College at Highgate, London. The Principal, Dr. Wardlaw, like Dr. Reynolds at Cheshunt, had a great influence on him. Here too he learned lessons in trusting God for financial needs, for he had no resources of his own and was very poor.

Before his commissioning and departure for Rarotonga in the South Pacific, he was invited to stay in the house of the Rev. Hugh Hercus and begin language study. There also he became engaged to Mr. Hercus' neice Jane, whom he had first met when she visited Glasgow in 1861. They were married just before his appointment as a missionary.

In January 1866, the "John Williams" sailed from Gravesend. Williams had been the L.M.S. pioneer missionary in Polynesia, martyred at Erromanga in 1839. Both the original and this second ship of the same name had been built from the offerings of Sunday School children. She was a large sailing ship with an auxiliary engine.

Hardly had they got half-way down the Channel when a fierce gale sprang up, and they lost some of the rigging and had to put in at Weymouth for repairs. All went well after that, and Australia was reached after several months. Immediately the party began a short tour of supporting churches. In August they set out for the New Hebrides group of islands. Sailing along on a clear sea, the ship suddenly ran aground on an underwater reef and began to leak badly. Only great labour with tow ropes and pumps saw them off the reef and back to Sydney; to the surprise of their friends! This time the repairs took six weeks.

They had lowered sail and were sitting, on quite a calm evening, off the island of Niue, when it was noticed the anchors were dragging and they were drifting slowly towards a reef. Nothing the crew could do could stop her approach to disaster. It was raining, and this did not help the immediate rush to the boats. The last few had just disembarked, when with a loud crash and sound of tearing timber the ship struck, and was slowly pounded to pieces by the sharp coral. Chalmers lost every possession except the shirt and trousers he was wearing, and a watch given him by the poor people of Glasgow. He wrote home, "Do not for a moment suppose we feel discouraged; we have no intention of turning back".

Supplied with some goods by other missionaries, they could only wait on Niue for another ship. Chalmers, daring as ever, determined to try his hand at surf-riding on a plank, as he had seen the islanders do. Misjudging his moment, he found himself swept under a wave and thrown violently on to some large boulders. Eventually he managed to scramble above wave-level and was helped to shore, very badly cut and bruised after his fifth dice with death by water.

The only way they could get to Rarotonga was by first going on to Samoa, much further away. The one ship going there was owned by a smuggler and pirate known as "Bully" Hayes. Perhaps because they had few possessions to steal, along with another missionary couple, Chalmers and his wife took passage with him. Chalmers' frank and fearless character had a strange effect on Bully Hayes, as on so many others. When the missionary asked rather hesitantly whether he could start a service on board, Hayes offered to force all his men to attend! He later wrote to Chalmers (in words similar, as we shall see, to those used later by a well-known author), "If only you were near me I should certainly become a new man, and live a different life".

On May 20th, 1867, sixteen months after leaving the Thames, they finally dropped anchor in the lagoon at Rarotonga. The burly islander who was helping Chalmers ashore asked in Pidgin English, "What fellow name belong you?" In his broad Scots tongue he replied, "Chalmers". "Tamate!", roared out the man to his friends on the shore, and Tamate he remained to them.

Tamate was surprised and at first rather disappointed to find out how Christianized the island was! The dedicated labours of John Williams had brought a profound change in these people. There were many national Christians, with pastors and evangelists, among its population of 7000 or so. However, Chalmers soon saw that there were three things he could do. Firstly, he could counsel and encourage the native pastors and students, secondly the existing schools and Sunday Schools needed re-organising, and thirdly he could write simple commentaries on the Prophets and Epistles. In all this he was to be helped by his wife.

Looking around as he polished up his knowledge of the language, he noticed that most of the young men did not attend worship. He found out that they spent Sundays drinking orange wine and rum together in forest clearings. Since his days in Glasgow, and even from his strict home background, Chalmers had always been a great total abstinence man, and he decided to advocate that here in Rarotonga. Other missionaries thought him extreme, but he pressed on regardless. Soon he realized that if the young bloods had useful work to do, they would be less tempted to drink away their health and money. So he organized a kind of adult Boys' Brigade, with drill as the main attraction. Later the members were led on to other projects like rebuilding churches damaged by hurricanes, and classes for the three Rs and Bible study. Fellow-missionaries tended to be scornful of these "para-military exercises"; and probably only Chalmers could have carried them off successfully.

As recreation, when he became tired of writing his commentaries and history book, he would go climbing up one of the steep peaks, or swimming in the lagoon. Soon he had another near fatal accident when he stumbled off the edge of the reef into the boiling surf; to be rescued by an islander who grabbed him by the hair as he was being sucked down by the undertow.

An indication of how popular he was came when they had been on the island less than a year. He had gone to the other side of the island to explore the possibility of living there, but had finally decided to settle at Avarua the landing place. One day a large crowd of natives arrived and began shouting loudly that the missionary should come and live with them on the other coast, not "among these bad people" in Avarua. Sensing that an argument might develop into a fight, Chalmers allowed himself to be carried off and spent several days there before quietly persuading them he must go back to Avarua, but would visit them frequently.

With all these activities, and editing an island newspaper too, Chalmers and his wife spent ten happy years on Rarotonga, saddened only by the news from Scotland that his aged father had died. The missionaries began to feel the work had reached the stage where it could be carried out largely by national Christians. Did they not have such men as Teava, a former cannibal hunter, who had gone as a missionary to Samoa? Many others were equally mature and devoted soldiers of the Cross. For a born pioneer like James Chalmers, the time to move on had come. Some evangelists from Rarotonga had recently gone as far as New Guinea, and it was to this second largest island in the world that the Chalmers' went also.

At that time the Western part was a colony of Holland, while Britain and Germany were still fencing over the Eastern half. Only the South coast of this part, known as Papua, had been explored. Of the interior, all that was known was that there were very long rivers (such as the Fly), vast grassy valleys and extensive rainforests, which had never known plough or axe. The people were fearsome head hunters constantly warring amongst themselves. As an early biographer wrote, it was still the Stone Age in Papua.

Mrs. Chalmers, whose health had been good on Rarotonga, faced the climate as well as the degradation of Papua with remarkable courage. Not long after they arrived, she was offered, as a mark of esteem, a piece of ready-cooked human flesh! Tamate himself was often in danger as he tried to arbitrate between tribes. On several occasions, only his cool approach and quick wits saved him. Consider the kind of people he was dealing with, as depicted by Alexander Small:

"A live Papuan in 'high-dress' was indeed a fearsome sight. He had a huge shock of frizzy hair which was crowned by a plume of cassowary or bird-of-paradise feathers almost doubling his height; he carried a spear; he wore an ornament of the size and shape of a pencil stuck through the septum of his nose; his ear lobes were perforated and distended to accommodate heavy shell or bamboo ornaments. He wore a waist belt of shells, a band of cowrie shells round his forehead, and shell armlets and anklets. He was extensively tattooed, and painted with fancy stripes of black or yellow or scarlet paint. His teeth and lips were so stained with betel-nut juice that they seemed to be dyed in blood. Of what we call clothing he wore nothing, and he rarely washed. He was a strange compound of cruelty, vice, superstition, and ignorance. He had developed thieving into a fine art, and was completely under the domination of the sorcerer. All sickness was regarded as witchcraft, and in every case of illness a victim had to be found to appease the deities".

For reasons both of safety and ventilation, the houses were built on trees with retractable ladders. In the middle of each village was a communal longhouse, the Dubu. It was used not only for palavers, but also for revolting religious and magical rites. The Chalmers' were constantly having things stolen, and only a firm patient politeness enabled them to keep their tempers - and their heads. God was surely looking after them.

It was not long before Chalmers was respected and held in some affection, and the Chief offered him his own daughter, saying Chalmers would never become a great man with only one wife!

On one occasion he announced his intention of going to visit a neighbouring tribe, the sworn enemies of his own village. The neighbours were horrified. They produced many skulls of the other tribe, to impress upon him that his own skull would be a good down payment on the revenge! But with a tribal teacher he set out along the coast to the village in question. A large whooping crowd rushed to his boat and hustled him ashore shouting "Goira, goira!". He feared he was going to die. After being rushed through the jungle to a clear bubbling spring, he finally understood they were speaking of water, not blood. One of the tribe then asked him in Pidgin to come and stay with them and build a house near this source of fresh water.

His dress caused wonder and a little fear, as he usually wore white and a topee, not the regulation missionary black with stove-pipe hat. Taking off his boot one day he saw the people scatter screaming. Here was a man whose foot screwed off; surely powerful magic!

His approach to strangers was by barter and gift. We may fault his saying that it was the gospel of tomahawks and tobacco that could alone be preached first - but it worked. His own chief was now on his side more and more, and this was seen in a rather frightening incident concerning Chalmers' own ship, the "Mayri". Seeing some natives trying to cut the anchor rope, one of the crew fired three times. Immediately more canoes approached the ship, and the occupants boarded her, injuring the captain and having one of their own men killed. An ugly situation arose, and Chalmers and his wife were threatened with death by an angry tribe. After praying most the night, they decided to stay, while the crew of the "Mayri" sailed off.

Soon a party from a neighbouring tribe arrived to assist in killing and eating the missionary couple. When they approached the house Chalmers went out and faced them with a gun in his hand, asking what harm he had done them, and telling them that as he was not going to give them any compensation, they had better go away. So compelling was his eye, and so watchful his God, that they returned to the nearby village and began quarreling among themselves. Eventually the visitors departed, shouting that they would return to kill not only Chalmers, but his tribe too. The chief jeeringly told them that until they had a missionary to supply them with axe-heads, they shouldn't try! When Chalmers provided his people with goods to exchange and sell to other villages, his fame spread.

Jane Chalmers had contracted tuberculosis soon after arriving in New Guinea, and as there was no medicine and the climate was humid, her health rapidly deteriorated and she had to leave for Sydney. Chalmers left later when he heard she was seriously ill, and reached Cooktown in Queensland to read of her death from a paragraph in a newspaper. This more than ever increased his determination to cut his roots in civilization and devote his life to Papua. "How I long for more entire consecration to His service. O, to dwell at His Cross and abound in blessed sympathy with Him and His great work! God help us by Thy Spirit. We want the heathen for Christ!"

On a trip to another district he met a rarity, a sullen chief who would not accept his presents. Returning down the beach, Chalmers was warned by one of his crew that a man with a club was walking behind him choosing a moment to strike. Quick as a flash Chalmers took a piece of hoop iron from his bag, thrust it into the man's hand and grabbed the club in exchange!

In 1884, a new test befell his work. The territory was annexed by Britain as a Protectorate, and merchant adventurers of a most unsavoury type began to exploit the tribes. Chalmers delighted in scotching their plans, and was cordially hated by them as a result. The British government, however, respected him greatly, and he had influence in having the export of slaves and the import of alcohol, opium, firearms and explosives prohibited in the new colony.

He was continually widening his journeys and finding new villages in which to settle the national teachers from Port Moresby, and his colleague there, Dr. Lawes, referred to him as the Livingstone of New Guinea. One of the missionaries from Rarotonga was killed by a warlike tribe, and the government reacted (against the missionaries' advice), by sending in a party of marines to demand satisfaction. The chief proving arrogant and threatening, the marines opened fire and killed him and several others. The tribe was immediately brought to submission and Chalmers called on later to make peace, and eventually a church was founded there.

Steadily his work of example, exhortation and teaching began to change the face of the territory and draw people to Christ. Like the more sophisticated of Athens, "When they heard of the resurrection of the dead, some mocked, others said 'we will hear you again on this'...but some joined him and believed".

Those who did respond were formed into churches. Chalmers' wisdom is seen in the way he never imposed Western culture on the tribespeople unless their own customs were definitely anti-Christian. So, for example, they wore the same loin-cloths as before instead of being forced to change to shirts, trousers or hats. Only the teachers wore such clothes, as a symbol of their authority.

Tamate's instruments such as thermometer, barometer, compass or even scissors were a subject of great awe and wonder to people who had never seen such things. However his social contacts were not always so light-hearted:

"Friends", said Tamate at length, "it is true I have come a long way to see you, on a moon when no-one has ever ventured to come before".

Grunts of approval resounded through the Dubu.

"I was warned not to come, for the men of Motumotu had sworn to kill me. I did not believe it, so I came, and we are friends".

"It is true Tamate, it is true", they cried.

"Very well then; whoever is your friend is my friend, and whoever is my friend is your friend".

"It is right, Tamate", came the response.

Chalmers paused. His bead-like eyes were on the Motumotuans.

"Kabadi is my friend. You must not go there again".

The supreme moment had arrived. It was his will or the will of the savages that must prevail. Unflinchingly Chalmers stood waiting the outcome of the issue.

"Speak, Raho! Is it peace?"

"It is all right, Tamate, it is peace; we will not go again to Kabadi".

Apart from such dangers to life, there were grave risks in sailing the mission boats around the coast and up the navigable rivers. Often it was only the help of friendly locals that enabled the crew to avoid sunken coral and beach in safety.

At last, in 1886, after more than twenty years of unbroken work, Chalmers agreed to a furlough. Despite his fears that he was uncouth and unfitted for polite society, his impact was great. At one place his fascinated audience heard him say, "I have had twenty-one years experience among natives...but I have never met a man or woman, or a single people, that your civilization without Christianity has civilized. Gospel and commerce; but remember it must be the Gospel first". And this: "The word 'sacrifice' should never be used by anyone who is serving Christ, and who could appreciate the sacrifice of Christ for us". He intensely disliked anyone making too much of his hair-raising adventures.

During his leave he was offered a post in the government of New Guinea, but refused it. He did however gladly attend a function arranged in his honour at Inverary Castle by the Duke of Argyll... He also found time to write a little book called "Pioneering in New Guinea", which was read by Robert Louis Stevenson among many others. Stevenson had previously been anti-missionary, but the book made him decide to meet Chalmers and see his work for himself.

The missionary sailed again for Australia in June 1887. With no children of his own, Chalmers always enjoyed their company, and was soon organising deck-games and generally romping about. In his more serious moments he held services for other passengers and crew. One immigrant Irish family had reason to remember him, for when he found out how little money they had left, he arranged a collection for them among the other passengers. His informal services were attended by people of all religions on board.

Arriving in Australia, he was surrounded immediately by people who wanted to honour him and hear him speak. It was suggested he should lead a party to climb Mount Owen Stanley, the highest peak in the interior of New Guinea. Feeling that his work as a missionary would suffer, he declined and returned to Port Moresby. Not long after his arrival there, Dr. and Mrs. Lawes departed on leave, and he took over their church and training college. Soon he heard of the death of a rainmaker he had befriended earlier. The man had stepped in front of another who was to be speared, and received the fatal blow himself. He died murmuring a little prayer Chalmers had taught him: "Great Spirit of love, give me light. Save me for Jesus' sake".

On a more amusing level, he sent off a telegram to the L.M.S. Headquarters in London, asking them to obtain and forward, "One gross of tomahawks, one gross butcher's knives". This at first caused great consternation, for the committee jumped to the wrong conclusion as to why he wanted them.

Eventually the Lawes' returned, with a new mission ship, the "Harrier", and Chalmers was free of his responsibilities at Port Moresby. During his furlough in England he had met again a life-long friend of his first wife, who had married and was now a widow - Mrs. Sarah Harrison. Their friendship blossomed, and after his return overseas they became engaged. Chalmers now went to Cooktown to meet her, and they were married and returned immediately to Papua.

After a short settling-in period at Port Moresby they left for Motumotu, where Chalmers had decided to settle. This was a dreadful trip for the new Tamate Hahine, whose health was soon affected by fevers. However she and her husband often played with the children of the coastal village, and having gained their confidence and that of their parents, started a school. Remembering perhaps his days in Rarotonga, Chalmers had the children marching and saying their ABC at the same time. It was always necessary to do something lively and dramatic to hold the Papuans' attention, and Tamate loved doing that.

The difficulties of this period of Chalmers' life must have been extremely great. He was responsible for many villages along the South Coast now, and was also trying to make his wife's work easier, as she kept falling ill in the humid unhealthy swampland. One other difficulty was the fact that every tribe had a different dialect - Chalmers jokingly said he felt sure the Tower of Babel must have been built somewhere in New Guinea. Fortunately, many could speak Pidgin; which is still the trade language of independent Papua/New Guinea today. Although his hold over the Papuans was amazing, he still had to take his life in his hands on many occasions by rushing in to settle differences before they became all-out battles. Watchful as ever, he once noticed a man with a club creep up behind him in the crowd. He turned around and called the native to his side with a, "You can see much better at this side".

At the invitation of Sir William McGregor the Governor, Chalmers accompanied him on a survey of the Fly River area in Western Papua. Mrs. Chalmers was left alone for nine weeks, and as she was suffering from fever for most of the time, and there were storms and threatening crowds of young men to contend with also, it speaks much of her bravery that she saw it out. It also speaks of the respect she and Chalmers had earned even in that still uncivilized village.

In the summer of 1890, it was obvious she needed a change and rest. Chalmers too wanted to revisit Samoa and Rarotonga to challenge more nationals to come and help in New Guinea. Several of the original band had died of fever or been murdered. They went via Brisbane and were feted again, and then sailed on a ship to Samoa.

Robert Louis Stevenson was also a passenger, and was fascinated by the stories Chalmers had to tell, and by the personality of the man whose book he had already read. Physically and intellectually these two were quite different, yet there was an immediate bond between them. Stevenson wrote the Chalmers' a letter saying, "Oh, Tamate, if I had met you when I was a boy and a bachelor, how different my life would have been". And to others he wrote, "He is a big stout wildish-looking man, iron grey, with big, bold, black eyes, and a deep, straight furrow down each cheek... He is a man nobody can see and not love. Did I tell you I took the chair at his missionary lecture by his own choice and was proud to be at his side even for so long. He has plenty of faults like the rest of us, but he's as big as a church!".

The Scots novelist and the missionary intended to meet again, but Stevenson was settling on Samoa, and within two years was dead of tuberculosis.

On their return to Rarotonga, Chalmers received a tumultuous welcome, especially as he remembered the names of everyone, even those who were children when he was a missionary there, and were now in their thirties! He was deeply affected by it all, and when he went to comfort the queen of the Island, who had lost her son, he simply could not speak for emotion. A group of men from Rarotonga, Samoa and Niue agreed to go as missionaries to New Guinea. On the other hand he was very distressed and angered at the further inroads made by alcohol, smuggled in by unscrupulous white traders with disastrous results on the islanders.

Their ship was followed to Port Moresby by the new "John Wiliams", carrying the islander missionaries, and Chalmers immediately left to settle them in their new stations. Later on the return trip the "Harrier" was wrecked on the Great Barrier Reef, and Chalmers again escaped a watery grave by a hair's breadth. His wife, who had heard rumours he was dead, must have been overjoyed to see his bearded figure walk up the beach at Motumotu.

After another illness in Tamate's absence, which brought her near death, Mrs. Chalmers was obliged to leave for England. Immediately after the sad parting, Chalmers and his crew set off, with the encouragement of the Mission authorities, to open up the Fly River area to the Gospel. The delta of the great river already had a missionary, but the upper reaches were quite unexplored. Chalmers suspected this territory was just as fever-ridden as the estuary. Landing on an island up the vast delta, he was wandering, depressed and frustrated, looking for a suitable camping site, when he had a strange and wonderful experience. Of all men the least mystical, he suddenly and distinctly heard a voice saying, "This is the way, walk in it". His depression lifted immediately, and he replied, "If this voice is Yours, Lord, help me to hear and act". The reply came, "Fear not; I am with you, be not afraid".

His spirit uplifted by this word of the Lord, he pressed on through the muggy desolate jungle. Finding a village on a strand, he also found a man who immediately agreed to sell him a house-site.

A glance at the map will show what a vast stretch of coastline Chalmers was responsible for. From Saquare in the Fly estuary to Port Moresby were many villages with and without evangelists. Chalmers had to pay periodic visits to them, at the same time making occasional trips up the River Fly. Navigation was extremely difficult, and on one occasion they were overtaken by a large tidal bore which damaged the rudder and stern-post. Despite the rumours that the tribespeople were unapproachable Chalmers went to them unarmed, and again God protected his servant. However he wrote in his diary about the prospect of sending missionaries to the interior, "God knows there will be many Gethsemanes, and it may be Calvarys; but all for Christ, and it is well".

In 1894 he was called back to London by the Society, and had a happy re-union with his wife, now restored to good health. The cooler climate had the opposite effect on him, but he pressed on with a big programme of meetings, and was given the Freedom of Inverary.

In 1896 he returned to New Guinea, and with fresh missionaries from Britain to take over part of his vast "parish", Chalmers was free to superintend new work on the islands off the coast, and in the Fly basin. Several churches were begun and staffed, schools erected and taught. His wife returned in 1897, but died on 26th October, 1900.

A young colleague, Oliver Tompkins, arrived to join Chalmers in the exploration of the Aird River area, and on one of its delta islands, in March 1901, the pair, with ten national evangelists were treacherously murdered.

Several villages were involved in the plot to seize the ship in which the party had been travelling, and it was only after a punitive expedition by the marines and another with an official interpreter, that the heads were given up for burial, the bodies having been cooked and eaten.

Chalmers' story is so much larger than life,that only at its close have we felt justified in offering an assessment of this great man of God. The first impression is of bigness, in body, in sympathy, in energy, in devotion. Like all men who see with broad vision, and are practical rather than theorists, he made mistakes. His utterances, even on theological topics, were sometimes open to question. He was not a great teacher, only a great pioneer. He did not always see that to employ men to preach the Gospel is sometimes to put temptation in their way, and wean them from direct responsibility to God. However, anyone who considers the complexity of these questions will see the answers are by no means straightforward. Soon after Tamate's death, an evangelist from Rotorua decided to settle in that very village where the Christian workers had been clubbed and stabbed.

Such was God's work through a man who wrote in one of his last letters, "How grand it would be to sit down in the midst of work and just hear the Master say, 'Your part is finished, come!'"

Adoniram Judson

1789 - 1850

❖

The unusual first name is Biblical; he pronounced it
with the stress on the "don" part. Like many Americans, he was proud to trace his ancestry back to the
second wave of Pilgrim Fathers. Judson's own father, also called
Adoniram, was a Congregational minister in the State of
Massachusetts, where his eldest son was born in 1789 at the
little town of Malden. The father was a strict disciplinarian, the
mother, as so often, the greater influence. Abigail taught her
son to read when he was three, and the father was astonished
one day to hear Adoniram junior read a chapter from the Bible.
Like many children of church-going parents, he liked to play
"church" - but a boy of four who can conduct a service with
perfect composure is something of a rarity. In those days, we
are told, he was very fond of a hymn, "Go preach My Gospel,
saith the Lord".

Other children were born as the family moved to Wenham
and later to Braintree, Mass., before settling in the historic land-

ing place of Plymouth. His younger sister Abigail was particularly close to Adoniram, and has left behind several reminiscences of his appetite for knowledge, and passion for experiment and solving puzzles. He would never ask his elders for solutions to his questions. At seven, he was "found in a field, at some distance from the house, stretched on his back, his hat with a circular hole cut in the crown, laid over his face, and his swollen eyes almost blinded by the intensive heat and light. He only told his father that he was looking at the sun; but he assured his sister that he had solved the problem with regard to the sun's moving, though she could never comprehend the process by which he arrived at the result".

Not much older, he studied a puzzle in a newspaper, and sent the solution off to the editor. The local postmaster, thinking it was some boyish prank, returned the letter to Judson senior, who after examining the question and answer, patted Adoniram's head, and said, "You are a very acute boy, and I expect you to become a great man". He then bought Adoniram a book of mathematical problems (which the boy found were merely similar to text-books used higher up the school!). By the age of ten, he had mastered basic arithmetic and begun the study of navigation. At the grammar school, because of the battered old hat he wore, and his proficiency in Latin and Greek, he was called "old Virgil dug up". After school, rather than playing games, he would often browse in his father's library, or read novels or plays (borrowed secretly from neighbours).

No constitution could escape the effects of such a studious childhood. He fell into an illness which lasted most of a year. Unable to read, he lay in bed planning his future. His sister says these dreams, shared with her, were very fanciful. In turn he wanted to be a great poet, a great orator, a great statesman, and finally, a great divine, admired by all those who heard his sermons.

Then "gradually, and without him becoming aware of his own train of thought, his mind instituted a comparison between the great worldly divine, toiling for the same perishable objects as his other favourites; and the humble minister of the Gospel, labouring only to please God and benefit his fellow-men. There was (so he thought) a sort of sublimity about that after all.." This was as far as his thoughts were allowed to go. He was still determined to be a great man in the worldly sense.

In 1804 he entered what is now Brown University at Providence, Rhode Island. He was a year younger than most of his class-mates, but this only served as a spur to his ambitions, and he studied with fierce application. The presence of another brilliant youth, John Bailey (later elected to Congress) only made Judson more anxious to come top in exams - and he usually did. However, Dr. Asa Messar, the President, in writing congratulations to his parents, ended significantly, "I most heartily pray that the Father of mercies may make him now while still a youth, a son in His spiritual family, and give him an earnest of the inheritance of the saints in light".

In fact, Judson was drifting further and further from God. Becoming friendly with an attractive and cultured young man who read Voltaire and Rousseau, Adoniram was soon professing himself an agnostic. He was increasingly unsettled as he went on to finish his degree, and on returning to Plymouth set himself up as a tutor, only to close his school after one year, chafing at the restrictions of manse life and wanting to broaden his experience. However, during that year he had produced two books, one on grammar, the other on arithmetic.

His parents tried to hide their shock at his open unbelief, and his father gave him a horse for his travels around New England. He proceeded to New York, where he joined a theatrical company, mainly to get some background for writing dramas and public speaking.

On his way back, God began to deal with him. Stopping at an uncle's house, he found it occupied instead by a young assistant minister, who impressed Judson by his deep and serious godliness. Later, he stayed overnight in a hotel. His sleep was disturbed by the groans of a young man, critically ill in the next room. In the morning, news came that the man had died. Judson had been troubled that he could offer no spiritual comfort. He was horrified to discover the dead man was his infidel friend of university days.

Not long after his chastened return to Plymouth, another Providential event occurred. His father was visited by two lecturers from Andover Theological Seminary, who, perhaps assuming the son of a godly man would himself be godly, tried to persuade Adoniram to enter their college! At first he refused, giving the reason that he was not convinced of the truth of Chrisitanity.

He did another spell of teaching, but eventually it was agreed he would commence studies at Andover, not as a candidate for the ministry, but to seek to resolve his own doubts and confusion. This he began in October 1808. Matheson shows deep insight when he says, "His mind did not readily yield to the force of evidence, but his is by no means an uncommon case; nor is it difficult of explanation. A deep-seated dislike for the humbling doctrines of the Cross frequently assumes the form of inability to apply the common principles of evidence to the case of revealed religion".

Within six weeks of his arrival he had been born again, and enjoyed his first real Christmas with his delighted parents. In May 1809 he joined his father's church by public profession of faith. Like many who have struggled to defend their rejection of Christ, once committed he never again knew doubt that he was justified before God by grace through faith, and an inheritor of eternal life, through the merits of Christ, His shed blood, and His resurrection.

Immediately he began to experience times of rejoicing in spirit, and prayer became sweet to him. "God is waiting to be gracious, and is willing to make us happy in religion, if we would not run away from Him. We refuse to open the window shutters, and complain that it is dark. God has promised that He will regard the man who is of a broken and contrite spirit, and trembleth at His word. He has promised that they that wait upon Him shall renew their strength. The Almighty, the

Unchangeably Faithful, has made the promises. He is not a man that He should lie, and His arm is not of flesh. Wait then upon the Lord".

In June 1809 he refused the offer of a Tutorship at Brown University, for already he was considering the missionary vocation. A written sermon entitled "The Star in the East" described the progress of the Gospel in South India through the great German missionary, Christian Friedrich Schwartz. Judson read it, and was very impressed. Among other things he studied at this time was a rather romanticized account by a Colonel Syme, of his period as ambassador to the Burmese Court at Ava.

The spark of missionary enthusiasm became a blaze through the arrival at Andover of four other students, already committed to the cause. Samuel J. Mills, James Richards, Luther Rice and Gordon Hall used to meet at a hay-stack near their school, and pray for foreign missions. A monument still stands there at Williamstown, marking the birth of the mighty American Protestant missionary movement. Judson and his friend Samuel Nott joined their group. In February 1810, walking in the woods, he definitely committed himself to overseas service. The decision was not lightly taken. He expected opposition from his parents, who of course saw him as a minister in the homeland. Neither was there any missionary society for him to join.

At this time, too, he was becoming convinced he should propose marriage to a young lady-friend, Ann Hasseltine. He was careful to describe to her the dangers and trials of missionary life in as much detail as he could imagine them. We honour her acceptance of his proposal - no ordinary human love led Ann Judson on in God's will, as we shall see. Strangely, both his and her father agreed without argument. Mothers and sisters wept, but the young couple were firm. They became engaged and looked for sponsors.

They could find only the London Missionary Society in England and approached it, at the same time urging their own denomination to form a missionary board. This did begin its work in 1810, but could not promise adequate support. Judson was sent to England to sound out the L.M.S. on the question of a joint sponsorship. On the way across the Atlantic, the ship was captured by French privateers and Judson, speaking no French, was taken to Bayonne with the other prisoners and marched towards the prison. Speaking loudly in English, Judson began declaiming against his rude handling. Another American happened to hear him, and sidling up, quietly promised help.

After a few hours, the door of the cell opened, and the tall American, wearing a large flowing cloak, was shown in. Remarking that he could not find the friend he was looking for, he swept the cloak over Judson and left, taking care to bribe the jailer and doorkeeper, who could hardly be unaware of what was happening! Once outside, they ran to the docks and got on board an American cargo-ship for the night. Papers for his (official) release took six weeks to come through, and it was not till May 6th, 1810, that he appeared in London.

Although the American Board of Commissioners for Foreign Missions was also a largely Congregational body, the L.M.S. was reluctant to share a missionary with it. Instead it offered to sponsor Judson itself. He returned to the U. S. A. and stated firmly that if his own Board would not do its duty he would indeed go back to London. This goaded the Board to a step of faith. Several missionary couples were taken on and sent to India, Burma, "or elsewhere, as in the view of the prudential committee, Providence shall open the most favourable door".

The "most favourable door" at that time seemed to be Eastern India. After all, there were at least three Baptists working in Bengal; the famous trio of Carey, Marshman and Ward. So on the 3rd February 1812, Judson said goodbye (for the last time, as it happened) to his parents, on the 5th he was married to Ann Hasseltine, on the 6th ordained, and on the 19th they sailed in the brig "Caravan".

Perhaps he thought the Baptist missionaries would prove argumentative? At any rate, Judson began to re-examine the Biblical doctrine of baptism. To his surprise he came to the conclusion that the baptism of infants was wrong, and that professing believers alone should be immersed. For some time after he mentioned this to Ann, his wife could not agree. After all, it would mean resigning from the American Board and losing their allowance, apart from anything else! However, by the time they reached Calcutta, she too was convinced, and they soon decided they should take the step of obedience to what they saw as God's will for them, and were baptized by William Ward. Most remarkably, one of the other Congregationalist missionaries, travelling on a different ship, had quite independently come to the same conclusion, and he, Luther Rice, was also baptized. His health soon broke down, and he returned to the U.S.A., where very soon God used him to stir up American Baptists in the cause of missions. The Judsons' faith was justified and their support assured. Incidentally, the three Serampore missionaries were more surprised than anyone, as they had never even broached the subject of baptism!

Contrary to what many critics say, the British authorities in India, apart from sympathetic individuals, were never particularly favourable to Christian missions. The East India Company, which at that time ruled a large part of India, was strongly anti-missions. It feared that its exploitations might be revealed. Just a year later, however, the position changed when William Wilberforce persuaded Parliament a clause should be put into the Company's Charter, giving freedom to preach. But in 1812, the Company could order Judson and Newell and their wives to leave its territories.

They sought and were given leave to go for a time to Mauritius, an island in the Indian Ocean. Mrs. Newell died on the way. Though the island itself (a French possession) was a ready field for labour, they could not stay there; but where could they go? Despite fears of the tyrannical Emperor, they decided to go to Burma, where Felix, son of William Carey of Serampore, had settled at Rangoon. So from Madras they embarked on a leaky old ship, where Mrs. Judson fell ill. A woman who was employed to attend her dropped dead a few hours after the vessel sailed, and the baby born in such trying circumstances died immediately and was buried in the stormy Bay of Bengal.

The mission to Burma had already seen much of Satan's opposition, all of the six missionaries except Felix Carey having been forced to retire. The Emperor had summoned Carey to the Palace at Ava to inoculate several of his family, and he was kept there as an unpaid civil servant for about a year. So he was not there to greet the Judsons, as the sorrowful, depressed couple moved their belongings into Felix's house, to be welcomed by his wife.

After a short interval for recovery, they commenced language study, and came to see that the Burmese, though Buddhists, were by no means passive or fawning in character, but a strong, clean, proud race of Mongoloid type. Most however were rather idle, and the country's great mineral resources had not been tapped. Agriculture and fruit-growing satisfied their needs. Apart from the humid climate which made everyone avoid hard work, the language was without a dictionary and no interpreter was available. Although their teacher was intelligent and helpful they had to communicate by signs at first.

After about a year Ann Judson became quite ill again and had to spend three months in Madras. Then Felix Carey, rather rashly, decided to move his family and settle at Ava. On the broad River Irrawaddy their ship capsized and sank. Mrs. Carey and their three children were drowned and all their goods lost. Carey retired, a broken man, his mind permanently affected.

Judson himself recorded nothing of his doings at this time, but Mrs. Judson wrote to a friend, "My mornings are busily employed in giving directions to the servants, providing food for the family, etc. At ten my teacher comes; when, were you present, you might see me in an inner room, at one side of my ivory table, and my teacher at the other, reading Burman, writing, talking, etc... I have many more interruptions than Mr. Judson, as I have the entire management of the family. This I took on myself for the sake of Mr. Judson attending more closely to the study of the language; yet I have found by a year's experience it was the most direct way I could have taken to acquire the language, as I am frequently obliged to talk Burman all day. I can talk and understand others better than Mr. Judson, though he knows really more about the nature and construction of the language than I do".

Their son, Roger, born in September 1815, lived only eight months.

As usual, Adoniram Judson applied himself to his study without rest, and eventually his head and eyes began to give him great pain. He was about to go on a sea voyage for a change when Mr. and Mrs. Hough arrived, bearing with them a printing press in Burmese type, the gift of Mr. Ward at Serampore. Within six months they had produced two pamphlets and Judson's revision of Felix Carey's translation of Matthew's Gospel. Slowly enquirers began to come, and it was possible to start a Bible class for women.

Not till December 1817 did Judson leave for Chittagong on his "rest cure". It turned out to be something quite different. He fell ill on board with fever, and was rescued from his plight by some English residents of Masulipatam. After anxiously waiting for several months, Mrs. Judson had just decided to go with the Houghs to Bengal to escape a cholera outbreak and anti-British feeling in Rangoon. At the last moment she decided to stay and was there when her husband finally returned. The arrival of new reinforcements, a Mr. and Mrs. Colman, heartened them.

Judson's next move was to open a zayat or preaching booth, which doubled as a church building on Sundays. In 1819, the first convert, Moung Nan, was baptized, and proved a valuable helper. Many enquired, some secretly believed, but were generally not ready for baptism in public. On one occasion, Judson agreed to baptize two of the young men at night. His diary reads,

"Nov. 7th, Lord's Day - Perhaps Jesus looked down upon us, pitied and forgave our weakness and marked us for His own;

perhaps if we deny Him not, He will acknowledge us another day more publicly than we venture at present to acknowledge Him. In the evening we all united in commemorating the dying love of our Redeemer, and I trust we enjoyed a little of His gacious presence in the midst of us.

"Nov. 10th. This evening is to be marked as the date of the first Burman prayer-meeting ever held. None present but myself and the three converts.

"Nov. 14th, Lord's Day. Have been much gratified to find that this evening the three converts repaired to the zayat and held a prayer-meeting of their own accord".

Progress indeed!

In the New Year of 1820, anxious to have their work as missionaries recognised, Judson and Colman made the 350 mile journey to Ava, to petition the Emperor. Despite their having introductions from one of the Ministers of State, the Emperor refused them official sanction, after reading the first two sentences of a specially prepared tract, and nothing of the Scriptures presented to him. Haughtily they were dismissed, and returned to Rangoon in low spirits.

Eventually they decided that Colman should go to Chittagong and set up a mission on British territory, ready to receive any exiled converts, and witness to Burmese passing through that port. The Judsons would remain, to encourage the few converts in evangelizing their neighbours. In the event, Colman died and his widow went on to Bengal soon afterwards. Meantime the Judsons saw seven more people converted by the power of the Holy Spirit, but then Mrs. Judson had to be sent home to America, seriously ill. On recovering, she spoke at various churches and another couple joined her on the return voyage. A Dr. Price had also arrived, and his medical knowledge brought a summons from the Emperor. Judson, as field leader, accompanied him, with the idea of persuading the Emperor that a mission station at Ava was desirable. This time the Emperor agreed. Furthermore, nothing but local opposition had so far come to the Christians at Rangoon. They now numbered eighteen, and could be left in the care of new missionaries. The Judsons moved to the capital.

A very dark cloud of suffering and loss was about to break upon their heads. The Emperor wished to annex the Indian port of Chittagong, and a British army was sent to meet his forces. All the Westerners in Burma were now suspected as spies, although the American Baptist missionaries were careful not to take sides. As soon as the British Army captured Rangoon, the foreigners in Ava were all rounded up and questioned. Unfortunately it was found that Judson's and Price's allowances came via a bank in British India, and this only confirmed Burmese suspicions the American misisionaries were in the pay of the British. The two men were tied up painfully with cords around their necks and hauled off to a filthy prison. There three pairs of iron fetters were attached to their legs, and at night their feet were hauled off the ground, so that they spent the hours of darkness in a very painful position resting on their shoulders and backs. They had no exercise and little food, and the heat within the prison was overpowering, as the cells were packed with men.

In this situation they continued for a month, while Ann Judson made frantic attempts to relieve their sufferings, by giving money to officers and requesting an audience with the State Governor. For a long time she was able to "visit" only for a few minutes at a time, and all their communication was through a door. Mrs. Judson's mental sufferings were not all she had to bear, for she had to make the journey on foot each day and sometimes sleep exhausted outside the walls. Fortunately she managed to destroy all correspondence with England (where they had many friends), but most of their money was confiscated.

The Emperor's women relations, who had formerly been her friends, absolutely refused to intercede for her. The Governor called her for an interview, but only to keep her out of the way while her husband and the others were moved on foot to another prison. Judson, being feverish and with swollen ankles and skinned feet from the manacles, had a nightmare journey.

It was probably only the devotion of a Bengali servant who bound his feet and helped him along, that saved his life, for had he become unconscious he might have been killed on the spot.

One of the officers had come to jeer at Judson, and asked scornfully, "What do you think now of the prospects for your mission?" Judson replied, "They are as bright as the promises of God". This is faith!

Meantime, Mrs, Judson's difficulties were increasing daily. The heroic woman found herself without food on several occasions. A Burmese child who was helping her with baby Maria caught smallpox, and despite Ann Judson giving Maria an inoculation, the baby also contracted the disease. When Ann herself became ill, the future for all of them looked black. After another visit to the prison, she wrote, "I just reached Ong-Pen-La when my strength seemed entirely exhausted. The good native cook came out to help me into the house, but so altered and emaciated was my appearance, that the poor fellow burst into tears at the first sight. I crawled on to the mat in the little room, to which I was confined for more than two months, and never perfectly recovered until I came to the English camp.

"At this period, when I was unable to take care of myself, or look after Mr, Judson, we must both have died had it not been for the faithful and affectionate care of our Bengali cook. A common Bengali cook will do nothing but the simple business of cooking, but he seemed to forget his caste, and almost his own wants, in his efforts to serve us. He would provide, cook and carry (Mr. Judson's) food, and then return to take care of me. I have frequently known him not to taste food till near night, in consequence of having to go so far for food and water, and in order to have Mr. Judson's dinner ready at the usual hour. He never complained, never asked for his wages, and never for a moment hesitated to go anywhere or perform any act we required. I take great pleasure in speaking of the faithful conduct of this servant, who is still with us, and I trust he has been well rewarded for his services". He was certainly God's provision for them.

Judson was allowed out of prison sometimes, for one thing only - to take little Maria to any nursing mothers who could supply the milk Mrs. Judson in her weakness could not. As the British Army continued to defeat all excursions against it, and drew steadily nearer to Ava, hasty arrangements were made to use Judson and Dr. Price as intermediaries. They were now released and treated with respect, as those who would know the psychology of Britishers! Sir Archibald Campbell, however, would have no bargaining, but demanded reparations to the sum of 10,000,000 rupees in four installments, and the release of all Westerners. So eventually, after much to-ing and fro-ing, peace was made in the February of 1826, the missionaries having been conveyed beforehand to the British Army encampment.

Adoniram Judson recovered quickly from his terrible sufferings, and physically nothing remained except large scars on his feet and ankles. But the mental scars were worse, and periodically thereafter he would become deeply depressed.

Ann Judson's health was however seriously undermined by her sufferings and anxieties, and an ordinary fever carried her off at Rangoon on October 24th, 1826, while her husband was away at Ava. He paid sad tribute to her as "the first of women, and the best of wives", and indeed as a missionary wife she ranks with Maria Taylor and Mary Moffat for heroism and devotion.

Judson's grief took on a pathological character, and he would often go off into the jungles, where he had dug a grave for himself, and seriously ponder the idea of suicide. Eventually, with the loving sympathy and comfort of fellow missionaries, he recovered his mental equilibrium, and resumed his work.

Other couples were coming to join the work, and other stations being opened. One of the most promising was at Mulmein. From there the Boardmans began to reach out to the Karens, a tribe who seem to have been marvellously prepared by the Holy Spirit. They had a legend that a white man from across the sea would come with a book to show them the true God. Both in Burma and in Thailand the tribe has yielded a great harvest to the Gospel. Judson soon became involved also among them, when Mr. Boardman died, and had the joy of reaping. Two hundred and seventeen were baptized in one year, 1831.

Donald McGavran, missionary strategist, relates how in an earlier stage of his life, Judson had patiently continued to share the Gospel with his Karen servant, though the man had seemed dull and unresponsive. However, this man, Ko Tha Byu, did become a Christian, and while Judson was evangelizing the Buddhist Burmese and seeing only moderate response, his servant was witnessing to Karens, who began to turn to Christ in large numbers. So although Judson may have failed in terms of modern missionary strategy, by continuing to work amongst the dominant Burmese, his original perseverance with one Karen was used by God.

He continued with his literary work also, revising the New Testament and writing many other works of Christian education and apologetics. Despite all this activity, he jealously maintained his own life with God. Writing on the subject of prayer, he urged, "Be resolute in this cause. Make all practical sacrifices in order to maintain it. Consider that thy time is short, and that business and company must not be allowed to rob thee of thy God".

In April 1834. Mr. Judson married Sarah Boardman, the widow of his late colleague. At about the same time he finished what he regarded as the greatest and most demanding of his tasks as a missionary; the translation of the whole Bible into Burmese. Immediately, he began revising it! Here are his feelings: "Thanks be to God, I have attained. I have knelt down before Him with the last leaf in my hand, and implored His forgiveness for all the sins which have followed my labours in this department, and future efforts to remove the errors and imperfections which necessarily cleave to the work, I have commended to His mercy and grace; I have dedicated it to His glory. May He make His own Word inspired, now complete in the Burmese tongue, the grand instrument of filling all Burma with songs of praise to our great God and Saviour Jesus Christ. Amen". That prayer was answered, for the Bible has proved a priceless asset to the Church in Burma which today is without any missionaries, and grows by the power of the Holy Spirit, using the written and preached Word.

His still over-full life had at least reached a happy routine, translating, preaching and talking to enquirers, counselling national pastors. His family life was equally satisfying. Three children were born to them; Abby Ann, Adoniram, and Elnathan (named after his younger brother, who had been converted some years after Adoniram left America). However, his health was deteriorating by then, and so was his wife's. They decided to go to Bengal, but there it was equally humid and the new baby, Henry, died. They proceeded to Mauritius again, and after some months another son was born. The Baptist Board of Missions now requested them, for a fuller recovery and to compile a Burmese dictionary, to return to America. Only his wife's declining health made Judson agree to the proposal. On the way, Sarah died at St. Helena.

With three of his five surviving children, the sorrowing man, twice a widower, reached Boston in October 1845. It is a measure of his great humility that he thought anxiously of where he could find lodgings. "The idea that a hundred houses would be thrown open to him and that he would be a welcome and honoured guest never entered his mind". Yet of course his sufferings and dedicated labours over thirty-three years made him a hero to the Christian churches of America. He found the lionizing distasteful, and could not reply eloquently, for his voice had almost gone. "Through the mercy of God I am permitted to stand here this evening, a pensioner of your bounty. I desire to thank you for all your sympathy and aid, and I pray God's blessing to rest upon you. All that has been done in Burma has been done by the churches through the feeble and unworthy instrumentality of myself and my brethren..." At that particular meeting he had a joyful reunion with Samuel Nott, one of the original "Hay-stack" group of college days.

During a deputation tour, he met his third wife, Fanny, who was quite different from the other two. She was a middle-aged novelist, and her later accounts of his activities are very vivid. She also seems to have made a good wife and stepmother. In July 1846 they sailed for Burma.

Although the churches were flourishing, a new Emperor had acceded to the throne, and he was strongly anti-missionary. Despite this, Judson was permitted to remain in Rangoon, as a "minister of a foreign religion ministering to foreigners resident in the place, and a dictionary-maker, labouring to promote the welfare of both countries". But they soon had to retreat to Mulmein, from where his wife wrote: "The good man works like a galley-slave, and really it quite distesses me sometimes, but he seems to get fat on it, so I try not to worry. He walks, or rather runs - like a boy over the hills, a mile or two each morning, then down to his books, scratch, puzzle, puzzle, and when he gets deep in the mire, out on the verandah with your humble servant by his side walking and talking ('kan'-ing we call it in Burman) till the point is elucidated, and then down again, and so on till ten o'clock in the evening. It is his walking that keeps him out of the grave".

In November 1849, while being up at night helping Mrs. Judson with a sick child, he caught a cold which affected his lungs and was followed by dysentery. After some time he agreed on a long sea-voyage to Mauritius. The trip was rough, and he died on 12th April 1850, being given a burial at sea.

Such a life needs no further comment. "He, being dead, is still speaking".

Henry Merriweather

1884 - 1977

---❖---

H arry Merriweather, as he was always called, is
another link person to the present day. His long life
began on 16th January 1884. It spanned the lingering
death of colonialism, the triumph of nationalisms, and the
resurgence of old religions. The first era began before he was
born, and was accompanied by great revivals of Evangelical
Christianity. Harry himself was powerfully affected by the
movement which broke out with renewed power in Wales in 1904.
It was a time of clearcut issues and standards.

In North Yorkshire too, religion was a very vital thing. He was
brought up on a farm near the large village of Masham. Two
generations of his Wesleyan Methodist family had already given
missionaries to the Church. "What memories the thought of
that Chapel revives! Memories of great local preachers who
preached in the power of the Spirit in the vernacular, of praying
saints and hearty congregational singing. To this day", he wrote
in old age, "the singing of certain hymns takes me back, and I

fancy I hear them being sung to the twitter of the sandmartins as they darted in and out around the Chapel windows".

It was in the hollow stump of a fallen old elm tree in the cow pasture that the boy sought to imitate the great preachers of those days, using it as his pulpit and preaching "to the surrounding buttercups and daisies!". It was not only the sight and sound of preaching that impressed his young mind, but the after-church prayer meetings, "when the saints came to the Communion rail and poured out their souls to God".

By the time he was sixteen, the family had moved to West Hartlepool. "We had a family pew in what was called 'Big Wesley', a large Methodist Chapel that had been built in faith in the centre of the town. At that time there was much excitement because the great evangelist Gypsy Smith was coming to our Chapel for an evangelistic campaign. The Spirit of the Lord worked, and quite a number of the young men and maidens of the senior Sunday School classes were converted. There was a night when I should have been, but I was too nervous to come down from the gallery where I was sitting, and walk right through the Church to the enquiry room at the other end. Nevertheless an older brother (William) who was converted at that time invited me the following week to a Mission Hall to hear a converted barber speak. This young man was on fire with a passion for souls and when, at the close of his address he made an appeal for any who would like to decide for Christ to come to the front, my brother asked if I wouldn't like to go. I didn't need much encouraging, and accompanying me there he led me to Christ".

The change was real, and he plunged straight into Sunday School teaching and other service. He recalled his first preaching engagement "as if it were yesterday; another fellow who had recently been converted and I were to take the Sunday morning service. I forget my own efforts, but I remember how my friend gave out his text, 'I am the light of the world' and then hopping off one leg on to the other he said it again, then changing his position he repeated it, and then looking into the air he said,

'Friends, I've been preaching it over to the ornaments on the mantelpiece all the morning, but it won't come now, so I'd better sit down!'".

Merriweather was never academically inclined, but he had business ability as well as zest for life and great love for people. As a Bible teacher he was vivid rather than profound, but his gifts were outstanding as pastor and even more so as an evangelist. There was a simplicity and directness about his approach to people. He went into commerce first in Chesterfield, then in Manchester briefly, and back to Chesterfield. Everywhere his leisure time was wholly given to service for Christ. At Chesterfield, "Sunday began with a prayer-meeting at 9.30 a.m. followed by a Sunday School in a very tough part of the town, then home 2 miles for lunch, back again at 2 p.m. for another Sunday School session, after which a band of us visited the old people in the Workhouse for a service, then home for tea, then off to one of the many lodging-houses for which Chesterfield was famed, after which there was the evening service followed by a prayer meeting and we finished up by visiting the aged and infirm who were unable to come to Church. What happy days they were!" Strenuous days, too.

In 1906, at the Chesterfield Conference for the deepening of spiritual life, Harry Merriweather was powerfully affected by the message of the main speaker, a leader of the Welsh Revival. Also taking part were some members of the Ceylon and India General Mission, an inter-denominational missionary society.

In the final meeting Merriweather found himself "standing tremblingly... and yielding my life to God to go to India if He could use me".

Obviously he needed more theological and practical experience, so he applied for, and began in September of 1906, a two year course at the Bible Training Institute, Glasgow. At this point, God saw fit to test his faith and obedience dramatically. He felt suddenly constrained to send all his savings to a worthy cause that was brought to his attention, and was left without fees to cover his entry to B.T.I. The following morning, a stranger approached him in the street, greeted him by name, and after enquiring about his needs, offered to pay not only his course fees but his outfit and passage to India too!

With students from Wales, there was a touch of revival at the Institute. Much preaching was done in the streets. It was not always easy to attract a crowd. On one occasion, Merriweather recalled, "A sudden inspiration seized me, and taking the collapsible organ stool to the other side of the street I put my New Testament on it and covered it with my muffler. Then walking around it, every once in a while I would lift up one corner of the muffler and cry, 'Yes friends, it's true, it *is* there!'. This went on for some minutes and soon the street end was packed, and pulling out my New Testament I told them it was the Word of God that was there, the Word that showed them the way of salvation".

In these years Merriweather developed his interest in and rapport with children and young people by visits to Quarrier's Orphan Homes, Bridge of Weir, and in the Fresh Air Fortnights on the Firth of Clyde for slum children. On one occasion, while he was speaking at Quarrier's, thirty children responded to an appeal for commitment to Christ. One later became Principal of a Bible School in South Africa.

Along with two older C.I.G.M. missionaries and one other recruit, he sailed on 11th November 1908 and began language study at Satyamangalam, in the Tamilnadu area of South India. After about a year he was given the job of teaching young men to read their own language. Even here "We were anxious that the young converts should have the Word of God hidden in their hearts, so finished up with a time of memorizing Scripture verses and prayer". Merriweather as a single man was highly embarrassed when they began to pray aloud for a wife for him! One even offered to act in Indian style as a go-between in approaching a particular lady missionary who seemed to his eyes suitable!

One of the senior missionaries, a Miss Kenny, was also a great evangelist, and had had the joy of seeing several people brought to faith and freedom, including a demon-possessed Hindu priest-ess. In baptizing such converts, Merriweather became convinced he himself should undergo baptism by immersion.

In the following summer, his Indian friends' prayers were an-swered when at the hill station of Kotagiri he met, and the next year became engaged to, Geraldine Cranmer Beauchamp of the Church of England Zenana Mission. She was nine years older than himself and had been working among Muslim women in Mysore city. Miss Beauchamp had, to say the least, an unusual back-ground for a missionary. Born in wealthy circumstances, she was brought up on her father's estate "Trevince", Gwennap, near Falmouth in Cornwall. In "Our Own Granny's Story", written many years later, she told how she got her middle name. "One of my ancestors had been the good Bishop Cranmer whom the naughty Roman Catholics had burned to death because he wouldn't worship idols"! Her mother dying at the birth of a younger sister, the father re-married. The new stepmother treated Geraldine and her sisters with something less than affection or equality. However, they grew up lively girls, and Geraldine had no psychological scars.

When she was twelve years old, they spent an extended holiday in Ireland with their maternal grandmother, and with their Aunt Augusta, Lady Gregory. This well known literary hostess numbered among her proteges W.B. Yeats, who wrote his poem on the wild swans at her residence, Coole Park, County Galway.

On his first visit to his prospective wife's family home, it was a matter of both wonder and amusement to the farmer's son, to have his cases unpacked and clothes laid out by the butler, one of a large number of servants.

Good Anglicans of a rather High Church tendency, the sisters were all confirmed as a matter of course, Geraldine when she was fifteen. She felt she had always loved God as best she knew, and remembered vividly the text from which Bishop Speechly spoke at her confirmation, "Speak, Lord, for Thy servant heareth". The local vicar, Canon Rogers, once spoke on Jairus' daughter, and emphasized how Jesus had turned out those who were making a lot of noise. Billy Bray, the little tin miner who led the vigorous and rowdy Non-Conformist witness in that area, later met the Canon and said to him, "I understand ye do like a peace and quietness? I do love a lot of noise!"

Geraldine's Evangelical faith developed only slowly, and for a long time she had a low opinion of missionaries and their work. This impression she had first gained on a visit to Ceylon, where her sister had married an agent in the tea business. However at the Keswick Convention in 1904 she finally surrendered to God's call. In her Bible she had come across the phrase, "ambassadors for Christ", and suddenly realized the honour and responsibility of that calling.

The couple were married in 1913 at St. John's Church, Bangalore, and returned from honeymoon by bullock cart "at two miles an hour" to Gobichettipalyam, where a new church building had been erected, but where the congregation numbered only five or six! Steadily the numbers grew as Hindus came to know the Lord Jesus, and with a legacy of Mrs. Merriweather's they also started a boarding home for orphans. Some of the girls there also became Christians. Later this station became the centre of a large work with a school, women's Bible School, and twelve village preaching points.

Perhaps the outstanding contact of those years was Nanjappan. His (much later) conversion is a fine example of the principle, "Sow now, reap in God's time". Harry Merriweather could write in 1969, "In one of the villages I remember starting a Sunday School first in a village street and then in a thatched shed... One day, the seven year-old son of the village priest knelt down to accept Christ. A few weeks later the annual Hindu festival took place, at which the priest would come under demons' possession". The young lad at first refused to take part in the festival, but his father punished him and insisted he did. "Thirty years had passed and I was now in Gobichettipalyam again for a weekend of meetings. On the Saturday morning I went out to Nanjappan's village and when he saw me he warmly invited me to his house - the best house in the village. As we sat down there was an idol in front of me and a picture of his gods on the wall.

"I found his father had died and he was now the village priest. I told him how I had prayed for him for 30 years ever since he had knelt down in the thatched shed. Then I got my Bible out and reminded him of texts he had learned in day and Sunday School and I said, 'And you are still tied to these things'. He told me he was not doing the devil-dancing now; he paid some-one else to do that, 'but I *am* tied to them', he said. As we talked the Spirit of God seemed to lay hold of him and he said, 'I'll be done with them', and rising up from the floor he tore the idol down and handed it to me and then pulling the picture down he tore it in pieces. We prayed, and on Sunday morning he was in the front seat at Church. Then his wife decided and some months later I was invited to come to Gobichettipalyam for a baptismal service; eleven were going to be baptized, four of them were Nanjappan, his wife, his son and his daughter. He is now in our Bible School and had led, among others, another priest to give up his idols and accept Christ as his Saviour". There is a hand-written addition, "He has been an evangelist for many years".

Because of travel restrictions during the First World War, a furlough in Britain was impossible, and instead in 1917 they decided to go to the United States by the Pacific sea route. Although they had no contacts there, they were met at San Francisco by a representative of the Christian and Missionary Alliance, who helped them find accommodation in the Bay city of Oakland. They were rented a delightful cottage in the middle of an orchard of apricot and other fruit trees. It was owned by a Miss Cody, neice of the famous "Buffalo Bill". In gratitude they named their third son, who was born there, after her.

Merriweather then had the privilege of sampling American friendliness and hospitality as he was given speaking engage-ments in various places. "My life was greatly enriched during this year by some sweet fellowship with some of God's ripest saints in America; Dr. R.A. Torrey, Dr. James Gray ...Mr. McNaughton (who became the C.I.G.M's first representative in the States), and ...I had the thrill of hearing Billy Sunday". While in Chicago later, he also attended regularly the Moody Church, where Dr. Paul Rader was pastor. Not only was he helped by such men, but they must have recognized in him one on whom God had laid His hand. For when the family were ready to return to India, the Moody Church decided to pay their fares. It was also at this Church Merriweather was ordained.

On their second furlough in 1922, a Baptist Church in Vassar, Michigan also adopted them. Just after his 85th birthday, Merriweather wrote to Pastor Bertelsmeyer of that Church to thank them for continued support and letters over 48 years.

In his customary way, he included a thought on a verse of Scripture, and a poem. Under another poem, on "Worry", there are some notes in his handwriting about two men who lived in Grumbling St. and Thanksgiving St. respectively. This typifies his ministry and life - simple, practical, urgent, trustful.

Mrs. Mary Dawson (as she became), went out in 1922 and knew the Merriweathers for many years. She remembers: "Mr. Merriweather loved the Tamils and they loved him. He was always full of the joy of the Lord. I never saw him angry or put out. Full of jokes too. But a teacher of the truth and an evangelist

..."One of his favourite stories was this. He acquired a car during my second year there - an old Ford - no other car in the area then. One had to go miles to get petrol and needed to keep several gallons in tins. Mr. M. often preached in one certain village. The headman listened, but argued and would never believe. Mr. M. one day told him and others the story of the two men building on rock and sand. He was a good story-teller. He called the one man (in Tamil of course), Mr. Forethought, the other one Mr. Afterthought. He rubbed it in, the need to think of our future and of eternity. The headman listened but did not respond.

"The following week Mr. M. and an evangelist were returning from a preaching tour, and passed through this village. Just as he got there, his car ran out of petrol, and he had no more with him. A crowd gathered and soon the headman arrived. He was pleased to get his own back. 'Ah, Mr. Merriweather, you told us not to be like foolish Mr. Afterthought, didn't you? And now, which are you? You are Mr. Afterthought, and how will you get home?' He had a great laugh. Mr. M. made the best use of it and often repeated the story. He had to hire a horse and cart and send a man many miles to get petrol before he could go home".

The years from 1923 were spent at "Anthiyur, where we had a Boys' boarding Home and 12 village schools, the teachers being teacher/pastors. Here in these villages we saw a number of conversions. In 1925 we returned to Gobichettipalyam, then in 1926-27 we were back again in Satymangalam and in 1928 we were asked to go to Ceylon to oversee the work there for a year and had a blessed year in Panadura where we had the joy of seeing some Buddhists and Hindus accepting Christ. The boys were at Breeks School in Ootacamund and came to Ceylon for their long holidays. They had great stories to tell of elephant rides and chasing kobragoyas, teaching Dad to dive in the river mouth, visiting the ships from the Maldive Islands where Henry had hoped to go as a missionary. Later he sent a Bible to the Sultan". Henry the oldest son, since his first simple yielding to Christ at the tender age of eight, had always shared his father's zeal for soul-winning. Tragically he was killed in 1944 while on active service in Italy as lieutenant with the 4th Mahratta Anti-tank Regiment. His father wrote a booklet on his life entitled, "They never yield".

So the busy fruitful years passed, until in 1930 the Merriweathers returned for their third furlough - which was to last fifteen years! This was because of needs at the home end in Britain. These were the Slump years. Apart from two trips to the U.S.A., they were spent first in Glasgow and then at Mildmay Park, North London, where Merriweather was for almost four years U.K. General Secretary of C.I.G.M. Then back to Glasgow, and eventually when the War ended, they were set free to return in October 1945, without the now grown-up children, to India. Harry Merriweather did his work as an organizer efficiently and without complaining, but it was never his calling. In his own account of his life he passes over these years with comparatively little comment. However in a later issue of the Mission magazine, "Darkness and Light", he wrote this: "Little did I think that I would travel from Cape Comorin to the Himalayas and then to Ceylon, and all through England, Scotland, Ireland and Wales, and from New York to Los Angeles and Michigan to Florida in the U.S.A. and from Hamilton to Vancouver in Canada, and have the joy of seeing souls saved in all these lands. How true it is that He takes the weak and the base and the nothings".

As an evangelist, Merriweather was never on holiday. "What memories flood the mind at the mention of each of these countries! Memories of battles fought and victories won, victories that were won oft-times only after prayer and fasting. Memories in the home lands of churches visited, large and small, where young lives responded to the claims of Christ. Of homes, where I met many of the cream of the Christian Church, and some where I had the joy of leading members of the family to the Lord. Memories of sacrificial giving so that others in India might have the Gospel, that almost made me weep. Memories of groups of faithful praying men and women mighty in faith who have stood behind us and whose faith has been an inspiration and a benediction".

Mrs. Merriweather's tattered copy of the Book of Common Prayer and Psalms is a documentation, till now necessarily private, of God's gracious dealings with them as a family over many years, and of their great faith in Him. For example, Psalm 9, verse 10 reads, "And they that know Thy Name will put their trust in Thee, for Thou, Lord, hast never failed them that seek thee". The whole verse is underlined, the word "never" is circled, and in the margin are these words in pencil, "Bill has his

£15 intact for M.T.C. March 1930", and, "When we were at wits' end corner £10 came in from Miss McGill's legatees. 1st February 1938". Against Psalm 25, verse 22, "Deliver Israel, O God, out of all his troubles", is this, "Praise the Lord, He has! - every bill paid at March 1937 and yet no allowances for January/ Feb".

During the Blitz in London, while living in Islington, she wrote against Psalm 57 verse 1, "God's answer to prayer in enabling me to sleep last night. October, 1940". In days of great financial difficulty for the Mission as a whole, followed by the dangers of war and family bereavement, another underlined series of verses sums up their experience: "Blessed is the man whom Thou chastenest, O Lord...that Thou mayest gave him patience in the time of adversity...for the Lord will not fail His people, neither will He forsake His inheritance...in the multitude of the sorrows that I had in my heart, Thy comforts have refreshed my soul"(Psalm 94, verses 12, 13, 14, 19).

Merriweather returned to India as Field Superintendent, and in late 1947, after 39 years service, they retired from C.I.G.M. But not from Christ's service! The Merriweathers moved to Kotagiri in the beautiful Nilgiri Hills and soon were asked to take on the pastorate of the Evangelical Union Church there. Probably they never thought the appointment would last 23 years! This was an English-language church attended by some remarkable people. Apart from missionaries of many Protestant denominations coming up for the hot season, there were visitors from the Philippines (a grateful letter is preserved from a couple there), Malaysia, Ceylon and Pakistan. The missionaries were from Denmark, Germany, Switzerland, as well as British and American citizens, Australians and New Zealanders.

Merriweather often had them to speak in the services. But for some of his congregation, such as two girls from Mizoram, North-East India, there was a distinct sense of disappointment when someone else stepped into the pulpit. Wrote Chumi, just before she left for further education in the U.S.A.:

"Do you know, whenever I sit in the Union Hall to listen to you give your children's talk and conclude with a plea that they would give their hearts to the Lord, I keep reminding myself to tell you something - but I never get round to it. I think it was about twelve years ago now, when I was seven years old, that on January 1st, after the sermon, I went home and after thinking about it as seriously as possible all day, knelt down before going to bed, and in all earnestness gave my heart and everything I had to God, praying that he would guide me in all I did throughout my life.

"Miss Clark wanted me to tell you about it - but I was far too shy to do so. However now you know, and you can know that whatever it was you said on that Sunday twelve years ago, you moved at least one childish heart, and I do want to thank you. My love to your wonderful wife".

The Miss Clark referred to was one of a pair of English ladies of the most intrepid type, who after pioneering for 35 years in the Lushai Hills of Mizoram, and seeing a church built from head-hunting hill tribes, had retired to Kotagiri. They had brought with them several orphan girls, one of whom was Chumi.

In 1969, Merriweather wrote, "In January I had my 85th birthday, and (don't tell anybody) I was grumbling - wasn't there a retiral age somewhere when one could be free from all responsibilities, etc? I read through the Bible yearly starting at Genesis and had just got into the 14th chapter of Joshua and there underlined in red ink stood out, 'And now lo, I am this day four score and five years old... Now therefore, give me this mountain'; and I turned to see if there was anything more comforting and there on the next page underlined was 'and Caleb (at 85) drove thence the three sons of Anak (the giants)'. So pray that like Caleb we might wholly follow the Lord and see Him in our old age helping us to drive out the giants and possess all our possessions".

Both the Merriweathers indeed took every opportunity to serve the Lord in old age. Mrs. Merriweather wrote a tract in her 92nd year, just after the Six-Day War, titled "The Overwhelming

Minority - Who helped Israel?" And it was through a mutual acquaintance with Lady Gregory that they got to know Mrs. Patricia Rasterick of Trichonopoly, wife of an Irish railway executive. She became a believer and was soon writing to them about her attempts to interest her husband in the Gospel.

It was not only at Kotagiri they were active, either. their plan in going there had been to pay short visits annually to their old stations in the Tamil districts of C.I.G.M. Here again they saw much blessing. Let Merriweather tell in his own words the story of Paul Asari:

"'Are you a Christian?' The man standing on the verandah was startled by the question for it was soon revealed he was one of India's 'holy' men who had sought to earn salvation by works and penances, without finding.

"My wife and I were paying our annual visit to the plains in the cool weather, and a father who had brought his daughter back to the Boarding Home after the Christmas holidays had come on to the verandah to say good-bye to Miss Casley and Miss Archer ere he took his two boys on the fourteen miles to the Boys' Boarding Home.

"Not knowing who the visitor was I had asked him the above question and got the reply, 'No, I'm a Hindu'. I found him a very interested Hindu and asked him to be seated. Ere long he was asking most intelligent questions about the way of salvation and it soon became evident that he was under conviction of sin. While we were talking I saw John, a Hindu priest I had had the joy of leading to Christ a few years previously, coming in. He sat down with us and I asked him to tell our Hindu friend what Christ had done for him. John told of his life in Hinduism with all its frustration and how one day he had taken Christ as his Saviour and how his life had been revolutionized by that choice.

"By the time John had finished it was very evident that our friend was strangely moved, and when eventually I asked him if he would like to accept Christ as his personal Saviour he said he would, and soon the three of us were kneeling together as the Hindu prayed and asked the Lord to come into his heart and save him. After he had prayed he continued for some time with eyes closed and hands clasped in the attitude of worship. When he arose I asked him where the Lord Jesus was? He replied 'He's in my heart'. Once again we had witnessed the amazing miracle of conversion".

Here, Merriweather was only reaping where others had sown. Years before, even after his child had been healed of a serious illness through the prayers of a Christian in his village, Asari had reacted with the violence of a convicted man when the Gospel was preached to him. The sudden death of his wife and the need to place his children in the Christian Homes, again brought him near. On that very day, one of his sons had said to him, "What's this, Dad, we are all going to Heaven and you to Hell?"

On his return to his home in the hills, Asari broke all his idols and was baptized, taking the name Paul. He began travelling throughout Tamilnadu, witnessing to others, and being used in several conversions. After four years he died, still serving Christ.

On another occasion towards the end of his pastorate, visiting Bangalore on holiday, Merriweather met a man called Moses whom he had known before, and later went to his house, where he met the man's twelve year-old son. After conversation he led the boy in a prayer for salvation. That was the fourth generation of one family to whom he had ministered!

Geraldine Merriweather died peacefully in September 1974, only three months or so short of her hundredth birthday. Her son Cody tells how he remarked to her on a visit that year that she would receive a telegram from the Queen on her next birthday. Her immediate response was, "I would rather see my King Whom I have served and hear His 'well done'". No wonder that among their sons and grand-children are active church members and workers for the Kingdom of God. Their second son Bill was for some years a missionary in Papua, and a nephew, Dr. Alfred Merriweather, served with the Church of Scotland Mission in Botswana.

Merriweather himself passed away in his sleep at Brooklands Missionary Home, Coonoor, on 15th September 1977. Let us close our account with extracts from an article written by colleague Mary McDonald about his memorial service:

"Sitting in the Church, waiting for the service to begin, one was reminded of Mr. Merriweather's wide interests outside the Mission and the Union Church, Kotagiri. Hebron School, of which he was for many years chairman of council, was well represented; so was the committee which runs the Missionary Guest House - he had been chairman of that too. Many a tired or discouraged missionary coming up to the hills for a rest received counsel, and cheer, and courage to go on, from a visit to him. A beautiful wreath told of of the love felt for him by the staff of the Kotagiri Missionary Fellowship Hospital. On more than one occasion Mr. Merriweather and also Mrs. Merriweather had been cared for in that hospital, and he had been chairman of that committee as well. John the Merriweathers' cook for a number of years, and 'Tumbi' their gardener were also there, as were many local non-Christian friends. Perhaps most striking of all was the presence of three tall Franciscan friars, probably young men to whom Mr. Merriweather had preached Christ (as he did to everyone he met) by the roadside or at the post office when he was posting his letters.

"The service was taken by Mr. Bruce Sinclair, and the note of triumph never faltered either in the Church or at the grave-side. After prayer we sang the hymn that many of us associate more than any other with Mr. Merriweather:

> 'Ten thousand thanks to Jesus
> Whose life our ransom paid
> Whose blood a full atonement
> For all the world has made...'

1 Corinthians 15 was read first in English and then in Tamil by Pastor Gurubatham who is at present pastor at Gobichettipalyam.

.."As we stood by the graveside we were challenged afresh to serve our generation as Mr. Merriweather served his. We shall not see his like again. It was the end of an era."

Ion Keith-Falconer
1856 - 1887

❖

T he Honourable Ion Keith-Falconer had the most aristo-
cratic of Scots blood flowing through his veins. His family
motto (in Latin of course), means, "What were lost are safe"
- somehow appropriate. Ion's father, the eighth Earl of Kintore,
was a devout Christian and elder of the Free Church of
Scotland. Born in Edinburgh, Ion Keith-Falconer was brought
up mainly at the ancestral seat near Inverurie, in Aberdeenshire.
From time to time the family would occupy accommodation at
Brighton or other resorts in the South of England.

Even from an early age, the boy was notably kind and
generous. Almost naturally religious too, though this was no
doubt the influence of the Holy Spirit, already working in his
young life. Educated at first by a private tutor, he and his elder
brother Dudley were sent away to a preparatory school at Cheam,
Surrey, when Ion was eleven years of age. From there, he won a
scholarship to Harrow. He was known at the great public school

as a bright but not a brilliant student. In 1873, he did win three prizes, in German and Maths.

Another subject he took up for sheer interest was short-hand, in which he became very proficient. This independent streak showed also in his not trying for any of the more conventional sports, but taking up cycle-racing instead. His house-master recalled his courage in plastering the walls of his room with Bible texts. When most of the boys began preparation classes for Confirmation, he declined to join, stating that he objected in principle to bishops!

But the lad was no prig or kill-joy. He had a famous laugh at verbal humour, which seemed to take over his whole shaking body. In later life, his own after-dinner speeches were often extremely humorous; but always characterized by perfect taste and decency.

After four years at Harrow, being rather young to enter University, he was sent for a year to study privately at the home of a clergyman at Hitchin. Here, he concentrated entirely on Mathematics. For recreation, he cycled, or practised short-hand; or a new interest, the tonic sol-fa system of music. He used to visit the homes of poor people, speaking to them about Christ, but also prepared to relieve their most pressing needs from his own pocket.

While he was at Hitchin, his brother Dudley, who had been sent to Cannes because of his poor health, died of tuberculosis. This was the first tragedy in Ion's life.

When he began studies at Cambridge, he once again showed his individuality by deciding to take rooms in the Market Square, rather than living in Trinity College. He had great self-discipline, and a facility for concentration that no noise outside could disturb, until he decided to have a break and watch the busy traffic. Keith-Falconer was always interested in ordinary people.

Beginning with the study of Mathematics, he changed to Theology after one year. This was not because he found Maths too hard - he won a prize for that year. Rather, it was because he could not put his whole natural enthusiasm into the subject; whereas Theology, he felt, would be more use to him. A greatly gifted linguist, he was soon winning prizes in Hebrew and Greek, and later being introduced to Arabic too - one of God's "coincidences"...

Near to exam time in his final year at Trinity, his younger brother also died. Ion was devastated; but sat the examinations and came out in the top six for Honours B.A. His tutors remarked on his remarkable ability to penetrate to the core of a subject and set out answers with admirable clarity.

Cambridge days saw even more cycling. Though at 6'3" he was not the best shape for the sport, he had tremendously strong legs and won most of his races with a great final spurt.

He recorded times at various distances which were not only Cambridge University but National amateur records, standing for some years. In fact, till the invention of the pneumatic tyre, in 1888! For all his racing and marathon rides were done on the old-fashioned solid tyres. Not only that, but the first bicyles with wheels of equal size had not yet appeared.

These sporting achievements were well mingled with much post-graduate study in 1878-80. He was during that time made President of the London Cycling Club, a post he held for ten years, till he went to live in Aden. In October 1878, he defeated the professional two mile champion of England by five yards. This triumph was repeated the following year, when he set a new record, this time edging past the same John Keen by a mere three inches! Remarkably, the feat was accomplished only days after several examinations.

In 1881 he rode all the way from Land's End to John O'Groats in 13 days, taking a longer route than was strictly necessary. On the third day, "A waggoner seeing me about to overtake him pulled very suddenly to the wrong side, and sent me sprawling over a heap of flints. No harm done. Shortly after, a wilful misdirection given me by a playful Somertonian sent me two and a half miles in the wrong direction, so that I traversed twelve instead of seven miles between Somerton and Glastonbury".

From Morpeth northwards, he was troubled intermittently by a pain in his right foot. Nevertheless on the last day he pushed himself all the way from Tain to John O'Groats without a break, being a distance of nearly 90 miles.

A third activity at this time was his mission hall work. In the Cambridge suburb of Barnwell was a small theatre which had fallen on hard times. While still an undergraduate, Keith-Falconer and others arranged to bring the American evangelist D.L. Moody to speak there. In the event Moody could not come, but meetings were so well attended it was decided to continue them on a regular basis. In 1878, a group of students managed to buy the theatre, with a generous contribution from Keith-Falconer. He spoke at the re-opening, on "Acting; for God".

During this period too, he was becoming heavily involved with a work in London's East End. It had been begun by another remarkable man, Frederick Charrington. A member of the famous brewing family, Charrington on becoming a Christian had given up his claim on the family income (one calculation put his prospective fortune as one-and-a-quarter million pounds; and this was a hundred years ago!). He had settled in Mile End and opened a mission hall with the aim of reclaiming young criminals, drunks and prostitutes, as well as the ordinary poor people of the area. Keith-Falconer was, as one biographer says, "A Jonathan to Charrington's David", fully one in God's service, as well as a great personal friend.

Charrington's boldness in rebuking sin often got him into physical danger as well as later into a court case with proprietors of a music-hall, who charged him with harming their trade. One supporter wrote:

"I shall never forget the night when Mr. Charrington was taken off by the police falsely accused of disturbance outside Lusby's Music Hall... In the dark I could see one tall man, standing in the centre, head and shoulders above everyone else, and perfectly white: this was Keith-Falconer, who had been covered with flour by the frequenters of the music-hall".

It was shortly after this that he made the decision to quit competitive cycling. Due to enter for the University Champion Race again on a day he was to give evidence in court, he wrote to the organisers: "The race is safe with Dodds. I have made up my mind not to run, having started in the race spoken of in Hebrews, chap. 12, verses 1, 2."

On several occasions, Charrington repaid the compliment by visiting Cambridge to speak at evangelistic meetings. Keith-Falconer once persuaded a college servant to attend, and in private conversation with the man after the meeting, the forceful Charrington urged: "Down on your knees!". Thereafter he was known to undergraduates in Cambridge as, "Doyk".

Keith-Falconer's help was invaluable in two great efforts made by the Tower Hamlets Mission, as it became known. Firstly, the winter of 1879 was exceptionally cold. Many of the poorest had to choose between fuel and food. An appeal was launched for the casual dockers and others without regular jobs. In a period of six weeks, twenty thousand meals were given out, and several hundred families supplied with other necessities.

The second campaign was to raise funds for a new, much larger mission hall, to seat the many hundreds now attending meetings. Apart from giving about £2000 of his own money, Keith-Falconer circulated among his well-off acquaintances and others a printed appeal he had prepared, which is a model of clarity. Among several well-known men and women who became patrons was Mr. R.C.L. Bevan of Hertfordshire, later to become his father-in-law.

But Keith-Falconer was even happier meeting people individually and doing what good he could, both spiritually and materially. He sponsored one man to emigrate; and a taximan was so grateful for help that he offered to take Ion anywhere in London at no charge. He was greatly loved by the common people of Mile End.

In 1880, Keith-Falconer decided to study more Arabic. The best European teachers were in Germany, so there he went, improving his German too, but giving himself more work than if he had learned Arabic through English. Being a natural linguist, he made remarkable progress in what is one of the world's most complex languages, and soon had a good basic knowledge.

Returning to London, he made the acquaintance of General C. G. Gordon, later the martyr hero of Khartoum. Gordon took great interest in this gifted young man, and offered him a semi-diplomatic post in Syria. Keith-Falconer declined; already, it seems feeling the stirrings of a Divine call, though it had not yet become clear where he was to serve.

Meantime, he determined to further his knowledge of colloquial as well as Classical Arabic, by going to Egypt. He described the railway journey up-country to Assiut like this:

"I tried to read but in a short time the book and I got so filthy with the dust that I became irritable and uncomfortable and could not read. After lunching on a dusty chicken, a dusty bit of cheese, dusty apples, dusty ham, dusty bread and some wine, I laid myself on the dusty seats and had a sleep for a couple of hours, and shortly arrived".

In passing, it might be noted that under British rule in the country, neither the railway authorities (if they provided the food), nor Keith-Falconer himself, showed much sensitivity to Muslim culture in having both ham and wine on the menu! Later, he learned more about not offending religious feelings.

At Assiut, he stayed with a Scots missionary, Dr. Hogg, whose knowledge of colloquial Arabic he greatly admired. This was only one accomplishment of one who was rather typical of the all-round missionaries of those days. Keith-Falconer was much less impressed by Egypt, its climate and its people. He caught fever and decided to return to Britain early, though his usual hard study meant he had managed to learn a little more Arabic, even in the short time he stayed in the country.

He continued studying the language at Cambridge, as well as translating a famous book from the Syriac. In 1883 he was appointed an examiner in Hebrew, and later was appointed Lecturer in the same subject at Clare College. In the following year, he helped examine the Theological Tripos.

A career as an academic was now wide open; but a holiday in Cannes gave him time to think and pray over his future, and gradually he felt a stronger and stronger conviction that he was meant to go overseas to preach the Gospel. This happened some months after he married Gwendolen Bevan, whom he had met some years earlier. His decision seems to have been influenced by the going out to China that year of the famous Cambridge Seven, including his personal friend C.T. Studd. Another factor was his reading the life of Dr. John Wilson of Bombay. Missionary books seem to be dangerous to worldly careers!

Versatile as ever, he had also finished writing a book on shorthand, and was then able to take his first exploratory trip to Aden. Why Aden? He had read an article in "The Christian" by a Major-General Haig, about the need for the evangelisation of Arabia. The land of Muhammad itself was virtually closed to all Westerners, but Aden, at the bottom of the huge Peninsula, was a British colony. Haig provided Keith-Falconer with enough information to fire his curiosity and zeal. It was not at all a small country on the edge of things, but an important centre of routes, attracting traders and settlers from throughout the Middle East. There was only one Anglican chaplain and some Roman Catholic priests and nuns in the country; otherwise, Islam held sway.

The main town, now also called Aden, was at that period known as Crater, being built in the bowl of an extinct volcano. The only other notable town in the British territory was called Steamer Point. The name Aden (pronounced differently in Arabic; the British are notorious for mis-pronouncing foreign names) interestingly refers to the Garden of Creation. The land, however, is poorly covered with vegetation, being hot and dry most of the time, as well as very rocky.

Keith-Falconer, though he had private means, (as will already be very obvious), felt he should associate himself with a missionary society, and was accepted to go under the auspices of the Free Church of Scotland, his family's denomination to which he had always been attached in spirit. He took his bride with him, and they arrived at Aden on October 28th, 1885. One of his first tasks was to begin teaching his wife Arabic. He humorously commented on the frustrations of the language: "Arabic grammars should be strongly bound, because learners are so often found to dash them frantically to the ground".

After that he would study himself, and in the afternoon walk into the town and try to open up conversations with the locals. His knowledge of Classical Arabic made people respect him, though he was still not very expert in the common language.

The couple's home was used from the beginning to offer hospitality to soldiers from the garrison. But Keith-Falconer, as well as trying to contact all kinds of people on an individual basis, was thinking about the advantages of setting up his missionary base at a smaller place called Sheikh Othman, between the two main towns, and further inland. Part of the reason for this was the rumour that the Church Missionary Society were planning to begin a work in Crater itself, and he did not want there to be any overlap in such a needy country. But the main factors were that the climate was slightly less enervating, and that Sheikh Othman was a place through which passed all trading caravans to and from Arabia itself - a strategic location indeed.

Like many another pioneer, he concluded that medical and educational work would be the best means of reaching the community. Then he added to these, plans for a school to train skilled tradesmen, of whom there was a painfully obvious shortage. There was, he saw, much practical Christianity to be displayed, before the people's misapprehensions about the Faith could be removed. These had arisen not only from the Qur'an itself, but also from the immoral behaviour of resident Europeans.

After obtaining with grateful ease a good plot of land to build on, the couple returned to Britain in March 1886. Keith-Falconer spoke on the possibilities of the mission in Aden to his denomination's General Assembly that summer, enlivening his account with personal experiences. The Assembly gave him renewed support - though in fact he himself arranged to cover the financial needs, not only of himself and wife, but of the buildings and salary of a doctor to man the proposed clinic. James Robson, his biographer, remarks that this last part was done in a particularly sensitive way typical of the man. The money was to be paid by himself to the Free Church's treasurer, who then sent it on from Scotland as from the Church. The idea was that the doctor would not feel himself constantly beholden.

In attempting to find a suitable person, he turned first to his old friend Charrington, who knew several medics working in an East End hospital. A Dr. Alex Paterson was interviewed in London, but could not go at that time. Later, he did become a worker in the Aden Mission. Then Keith-Falconer heard of another working in Glasgow's Western Infirmary. They met, and it became clear that here in Dr. Cowen was God's answer, so at one were they in spirit; an impression only confirmed to the full by their short labours together.

During the period in the homeland, Keith-Falconer was just as involved as ever in a range of other activities near to his heart, including bicycling, and short-hand, on which he wrote an entry for the Encyclopaedia Britannica! He even decided to accept an offer from Cambridge University of a Professorship in Arabic, since it would not interfere with his missionary activities. It was something of a sinecure, involving only an annual series of three lectures. His hope was, it would give him access to new contacts in the Arab world. To the lectures he gave a great deal of thought and study. Illustrative of his amazing linguistic gift (as well as appetite for work, and thoroughness), was his deciding to learn Dutch in three weeks so he could read a book he had heard recommended! This book was on the Pilgrimage to Mecca, the subject of his lectures.

His biographer preserves examples of his speeches to various bodies, including an amusing recollection at his cycling club annual dinner of how a friend's dislocated elbow was reset by a local doctor in the North of Scotland, after a visiting London physician had prescribed long rest and other treatment. Like his Master, he was at home in any company; but often turned people's minds to serious matters before finishing his remarks.

He visited the Mile End work again, and made arrangements, in part by contributing generously, for the Barnwell Mission in Cambridge to have a full-time missioner. His agreeing to work in this with the local Anglicans, gives the lie to accusations that he was a bigoted Dissenter.

In addressing missionary meetings in Scotland that Autumn, he expressed a certain over-optimism about the prospects for converting Muslims. "As the Law to the Jews, so Islam to the Arabs, is a schoolmaster to bring them to Christ". Emphasizing those verses in the Qur'an that say Islam had come to restore the religion of Abraham, he neglected those which say Judaism and Christianity have meantime perverted the true faith of Abraham! And (to show how much missionary supporters have changed in the intervening one hundred years), he appealed especially to those like himself with independent means. They should give, not just money, but themselves to go:

"You will have added your own personal example, and taken your share in the real work. We have a great and imposing War Office, but a very small army....While vast continents are shrouded in almost utter darkness, and hundreds of millions suffer the horrors of heathenism and Islam, the burden of proof lies upon you to show that the circumstances in which God has placed you were meant by Him to keep you out of the mission-field". Echoes of James Gilmour!

Keith-Falconer departed Cambridge in November, hurried but at peace. He impressed many friends by this God-given attitude. "One of the most gifted, many-sided of the sons whom our dear mother Cambridge ever reared, had left her walls for ever".

His wife had already gone to Cannes, and on 12th November they sailed together from Marseilles to Alexandria. Gwendolen remained there while her husband met Dr. Cowen, who had sailed separately, at Aden. The plan was that she would rejoin them, once they had obtained suitable temporary accommodation at

Sheikh Othman. Meanwhile, she began learning colloquial Arabic and visiting homes in Alexandria with American Mission friends.

Earlier, a certain Hasan Ali had verbally agreed to let them another bungalow while their own was in the building. Now he began in typical Eastern style to ask for more money. Keith-Falconer, who could be very firm when necessary, refused to increase his offer, which he considered very reasonable. He realized that to pay more would gain him the reputation of a soft European who could be exploited. Unfortunately, this meant the two missionaries had to live for many months in a very inferior dwelling open to the winds. Keith-Falconer jokingly wrote that their address could be, "The Draughts, Sheikh Othman".

Nevertheless, he was quite undeterred by the disadvantages. Certainly they did not stop him pursuing a remarkable programme of work. It included further study of Arabic, teaching it to Dr. Cowen, and once she arrived, his wife, translating books, beginning to learn the rather different Bedouin tongue, elementary medicine (partly by translating for the doctor, whose ministry of healing soon began to expand). Later he began the study of Somali and Hindustani, to reach those in the country who were not mother-tongue Arabic speakers. Also, he learned by heart verses from the Arabic Bible and the Qur'an, to be used in evangelism. And on top of all this, he employed the building contractors, and supervised their work almost daily.

Dr. Cowen and he took two trips up-country to explore possibilities for later extension, and because of the medical help they brought, were warmly welcomed and allowed to distribute portions of Scripture. These villages were outside the British protected area, in Yemen proper. He had opportunities to help poor individuals in very practical ways, as he loved to do.

In the midst of such encouraging beginnings, both the Keith-Falconers and Dr. Cowen began to fall victim to fever. It was not yet known that malaria is caused by mosquito bites, and the same draughts that blew these insect pests into the house, also hindered recovery. After several bouts, Ion Keith-Falconer had by February 1887 become very weakened.

So the couple left Sheikh Othman for Khor Maksar to recuperate with friends. But already, the fever seemed to have him in a spasmodic but firm grip. By the end of April, he was still in a low state of body. Sadly, his characteristic optimism was quite misplaced, when he wrote to his mother:

"You need not have the slightest concern about us. At the present moment we are distinctly better than we were after the first attack. We are not being gradually worn out".

On 5th May, a visit to inspect progress on the buildings did wear him out, and brought another relapse. Showing his usual concern for others and for the work, he insisted Dr. Cowen proceed with his plans of returning to Britain in June to obtain equipment for his work.

On 10th May, Ion Keith-Falconer died peacefully in his sleep. His work lived on; indeed it grew and developed, by the coming of several workers inspired by his life and ministry.

Nevertheless, we are tempted to ask, though not, we hope, with the lack of spiritual insight of the original disciples of Jesus; "Why this waste?" Why did such a talented, dedicated servant of God have to die so young, at the near beginning of his missionary life? Perhaps the only hint of an explanation outside the sometimes mysterious providence of God, is that he was essentially a vision person. Like Allen Gardiner, he was an initiator of work that needed to be continued by others with different gifts and less imagination. Not that he lacked perseverance; but such was his wealth of talents that he could hardly have remained for years in just one sphere of service. Be that as it may, Ion Keith-Falconer is one more example of the "many-sided grace of God" seen through human lives surrendered to Him. He did his part; he used all of his "five talents". No-one can do more.

Amy Carmichael

1867 - 1951

❖

Anyone trying to assess this great but complex missionary should read two full-length biographies. The first is by Bishop Frank Houghton, of the C.I.M. (also a fine hymn-writer). Dated 1953 and long out of print, it is the work of one who whole-heartedly admired his subject, but was quite reticent about some negative aspects of her life. The other is by Elisabeth Elliot, dated 1987, and is more "modern", probing, but in places, a little speculative.

Amy was born at Millisle, on the County Down coast of what is now Northern Ireland. Her family were of Scots origin and owned a flour-mill. Both her parents were fine Christians and Presbyterians, morally uncompromising but allowing considerable freedom to the seven children to play around the sea-shore and village. It was a happy, open-air upbringing. The family were known as good employers, caring for workers in practical ways.

Even from childhood, Amy displayed leadership qualities, and not just because she was the eldest. Certain stories (related in her books) have become well-known, such as the time when she prayed that God would give her blue eyes, and was terribly disappointed when they remained stubbornly brown. Later, on at least one occasion, her brown eyes were a distinct advantage. Then there was the time when she led the other children on a walk along the edge of the house-roof. And the time when, in a little boat on fast-running Strangford Lough, they were rescued from danger of drowning because coastguards heard them singing!

Amy was always sympathetic and helpful by nature. But she could also be quite strong-minded with those she disliked. Perhaps it was her slightly tomboyish nature that persuaded her parents to send her to boarding-school in Harrogate, York-shire for three years. She did not at all enjoy this time away from home and subject to strict discipline. But it was here, during a children's mission run by the C.S.S.M., that God confirmed His work of grace in her heart.

She returned to Belfast, where her parents had moved to re-start their now declining business, and studied music, singing and painting. In their new home, many of the well-known Christian speakers of the day were entertained and listened to. But a large loan never repaid to him seriously affected David Carmichael's health, as well as his business, and he died of pneumonia when Amy was just 17.

Immediately, she began to help care for the younger siblings, as well as being a strength to her devastated Mother. Her younger sister later wrote: "She was always able to see the positive and ignore the negative, and once she had an object before her which she was convinced was worth working for, no difficulty in the way could deter her". A good summary of her character, as we shall see again and again!

It was during this time that Amy had one of her almost mystical experiences. One Sunday morning, helping a poor old woman along a street in Belfast, past crowds of respectable worshippers who stared, she heard a voice quoting the Bible. "Gold, silver, precious stones, wood, hay, stubble - every man's work shall be made manifest; for the Day shall declare it, because it shall be declared by fire, and the fire shall try every man's work, of what sort it is. If any man's work abide... ". The desire to do only the purest and most lasting work for God, whatever others thought, was born in her. A desire, that sometimes caused misunderstanding with fellow-workers in the years ahead. This event led also to a decision to wear only plain clothes, not fashionable ones.

Amy was now in contact with more poverty and immorality than she had ever seen in Millisle or Harrogate. Working briefly with the Belfast City Mission, she determined to start a work for the mill-girls or "shawlies". She simply asked one of the mill owners for some spare land, but decided not to ask for any money to maintain the work she was beginning. A kind friend, unasked, gave the whole cost of erecting a hall. It still stands today as a little church on Cambrai Street, between the now well-known thoroughfares of Shankill and Crumlin Roads.

The work was named "The Welcome", and Amy's principle of resources received by faith and prayer alone was firmly established. She was only twenty at the time, and in the next two years, spearheaded a growing work. It was then handed over to lieutenants, because the family's finances had reached a final crisis. The house could no longer be kept on, all four of the boys had to emigrate, and two of the three daughters accompanied their Mother to a new life in Manchester. There, both Amy and Mrs. Carmichael were given small salaries by the Manchester City Mission. Amy's work was rather similar to that at The Welcome; her Mother supervised a Rescue Home.

It was Amy's characteristic enthusiasm and zeal, making her neglect simple necessities like food, that made her ill, and she had to give up the work after only a year or so. During the last few years, since he had first visited them in Belfast, Robert Wilson, the Quaker businessman and co-founder of the Keswick Convention, had often hosted them for holidays at his residence,

Broughton Grange in Cumbria. Now he asked Amy to live there long-term, as a replacement for his only daughter, who had died in the same year as David Carmichael.

It was a a strange situation to come into. Wilson's sons were much older than Amy, set in their ways, and initially resented the vivacious young woman who now shared their father's deep affection. For Amy it was a time to exercise her tact as well as enthusiasms. It was also a time of learning, especially in terms of the Keswick Convention's message of holiness and Christian unity. So very clearly, God was preparing her for her life's work on inter-denominational and devotional lines.

She was privileged to meet many more of the spiritual giants of the day; Hudson Taylor (for whom she had a special affinity), Theodore Monod, Reginald Ratcliffe, F.B. Meyer, Bishop Handley Moule and others.

On a snowy evening in January 1892, Amy became aware, apparently within a relatively short time, that God was about to stir up her nest again. It was a call to missionary service. This caused her considerable anxiety as she thought of the implications, both for her own family and for the "Dear Old Man", as they called him, so dependent on her emotionally.

The letters between her Mother, Robert Wilson, and Amy show a wonderful resignation and willingness to sacrifice on the part of the former two. Amy's great strength of character shows plainly, especially as she still had little idea where she was to go. After some months of confusion, she settled on China, and applied to the China Inland Mission.

Failing its medical examination was the second test of her calling. It is in a way surprising that the Convention, which had just that year decided to sponsor its own missionaries, took on her support. Her departure anywhere was delayed by a full year, then she decided to go to Japan. Typically certain of God's leading, she left with three returning missionaries before receiving acceptance of this plan by Barclay Buxton, leader of the work she planned to join!

Arriving at Shanghai with the C.I.M.ers, she found a letter from him welcoming her. "This leap in the dark is a leap into the sunshine after all". The sunshine was dimmed by a conversation with an older fellow-missionary, who seemed surprised Amy thought missionaries always lived in love for each other. Another firm foundation stone was laid that day for her own work in later years; the maintenance of love as primary. Buxton's mission was less highly organised than the older C.I.M., and language learning (though Japanese IS very difficult) took a back seat to evangelising through native interpreters. Remarkably, Amy's preaching bore fruit in conversions almost immediately. In one village, they decided to pray definitely one week for one convert. Before the next visit, their request was for two. Then four. Then eight. All were saved, all stood. Imagine the confirmation this must have been to her calling; not that she was ever inclined to doubt it.

On one occasion, a demon-possessed man was delivered. From such experiences, she learned lessons often to be proved foundational. To pray through to victory, to "show" as well as tell the power of Christ. Other lessons were perhaps more controversial at the time, such as her refusal to use any pictures of Christ (nearly all missionaries did), and her adoption of only national dress. Both these she later made part of the Pattern for Dohnavur.

It appears (though she was very reticent about the details) that at this time she received the first of two proposals of marriage. It did not take her long to decide, firmly as ever, that marriage was not God's plan for her. Incidentally, though she hated being photographed, such few as exist show a pretty, if not beautiful, woman.

During this time she developed neuralgia, a very painful condition that would affect her for the rest of her life. She was forced to have a break, and eventually decided, while in Shanghai, to go on to Ceylon, with a vague but firm sense that God had something for her to do there. The journey was a difficult one, but once arrived she found a little group of

Western women who welcomed her help, indeed leading, in their village work. Robert Wilson and the Keswick Committee wrote, very concerned at this departure without any consultation. Amy wrote to her Mother, that though she should have waited to explain before going, she was not prepared to agree to the apology for her hasty action which he suggested she send to supporters. At the same time, she refused completely returning to England for her health's sake. It was, instead, the Dear Old Man's sudden stroke that brought her home.

In these incidents, we see what could be described as stubbornness. More charitably, they can be interpreted as an absolute certainly of individual guidance. Often, her "guidance" was proved right by events. But not always.

Her ten months in England was one of the quieter parts of her life. She did write the first of many books, "From Sunrise Land", but was advised not to return to the tropics. However, sure of the call, as soon as Wilson was better she arranged to join the Church of England Zenana Missionary Society. This worked in the Bangalore area of India, a particularly cool and healthy climate. In sailing from London on October 11th 1895, she had, as it happened, left Britain for ever. Dengue fever welcomed her to her new country. But she soon recovered and tackled Tamil, another difficult language where several ideas can be put into one (very long) word.

The state of the churches in Tamil Nadu greatly disturbed Amy. "Baptised Hinduism" she called it, and again resolved to build her own work on no such compromises. She also became very outspoken about Western colleagues' attitudes and life-style, and wrote another little booklet about it, which did not endear her to the missionary community. When she produced the longer book, "Things as they are", some years later, she was heavily criticised for painting too gloomy a picture of the obstacles and failures. Not pessimistic, but realistic, she maintained. The churches of Tinnevelly district had, around the year 1860, experienced a great revival, associated with the work of J.C. Aroolappen and other Indian Brethren evangelists. But all too little of the afterglow remained, thirty-five years later.

Amy's adapting native dress and habit of galloping around on a horse further failed to impress the social establishment. So did her statement that holidays in the hills were a waste of time. Exhaustion after a hot summer on the plains showed her the folly of at least that opinion. One conviction grew even stronger; that she would never employ non-Christians or mere nominal Christians in any service for God. "I begin to feel like a fish out of water, and such a fish is a discouraged creature. One day, when this feeling was upon me, a letter came from a Keswick friend at home. 'Do not cool. Look to Him to keep you burning and shining'. That letter was like a drink of well water on a hot day. I can never be grateful enough for the tender mercy that brought it then".

One good friend she did make in these lonely years. Thomas Walker of Tinnevelly (correctly, Tirunelveli) offered to teach her Tamil. At first she found him stiff and scholarly. Later he and Mrs. Walker became her best friends and counsellors.

A near-fatal accident convinced her that her hope of going to Tinnevelly District to study and work with the Walkers was of God. She saw the accident as Satan's attempt to stop her. On November 30th, 1896, she left Bangalore for the southernmost part of India. Walker was a good teacher, and one of the few men who could tell Amy what to do. In this case, to learn the language before getting too involved in evangelistic activity. She learned quickly and well, and Tamil proverbs and phrases enliven her writing ever afterward.

Then she began evangelistic trips, initially with the Walkers, later with Indian women companions, around the large number of villages scattered throughout the area. When a Brahmin girl, Pappammal, was apparently converted, the Hindu community turned fiercely against the preachers. Worse, it later turned out that Pappammal was not genuine, but part of a plot by her lover to marry outside his caste. Amy was shocked. "The Eastern mind and soul seems to me like a cabinet of secret drawers - you never know when you get to the last one".

A more encouraging development in those years was in Ponnammal. She was the first among the Starry Cluster (as the lady evangelists were known locally) to give up her jewels, the security and status symbol of Indian women. Later she gave many other evidences of her wholehearted devotion, knitting her heart with that of Amy Carmichael, and becoming a trusted assistant in the later work.

Amy was learning more and more about the depths of cruelty and degredation associated with the impressive temples, and the religion practiced there. Several women had been converted, and children too, all involving persecution and refuge with the Mission. One of them was Arulai, who later became Amy's chosen successor at Dohnavur.

Some children seemed very difficult to reach, still less to reclaim. Gradually, Amy became aware of the fact that ritual prostitution was part of the temple worship. And that little girls were being sold to the temples by their parents, to be trained for this degrading role.

She had found her special work, though it developed with frustrating slowness. She was already being called "the child-stealing ammal (lady)", and indeed she had a rare influence of love upon children, who instantly trusted and responded to her. Gradually, as she explained in "Gold Cord", the truth of the Tamil proverb became clear to her; "Children tie the mother's feet". Amy found her itinerant work was coming to an end. She moved into an old bungalow that had been empty for years, in a village distinguished only by its dreariness, Dohnavur. And she prayed and prayed for more children to mother there.

In ones and twos, children began to arrive. Sometimes by their own initiative, sometimes offered for a price, sometimes having been rescued by sympathetic Indian Christians. The work was far from glamorous, involving as it did 24-hour care of young lives, and sometimes anxieties and griefs over sick and dying ones. "If by doing some work which the undiscerning consider 'not spiritual work', I can best help others, and I inwardly rebel, thinking it is the spiritual for which I crave, when in truth it is the interesting and exciting; then I know nothing of Calvary love". This quotation from one of her books shows her deep dedication to whatever task God gave her, and her emphasis on serving out of love, not out of duty, or desire for reward, recognition or fulfillment.

In 1901, just as the new work was developing, another accident befell Amy and some of the girls. Off Cape Comorin, sailing in a catamaran, they were swept overboard by a big wave. All were rescued; surely God's preservation of His work against a crude Satanic attack.

In 1905, her Mother was able to visit from the U.K., and it was also in that year that a touch of revival affected the girls, deepening their experience of God. Cholera also visited the area, though none of the house's children were infected, despite Amy and others having to go in and out of the compound helping others.

In 1908 she wrote yet another book, "The Beginning of a Story", which recounted God's provision for them. True to her principles, she did not ask for money, even deleting one sentence which mentioned the word. She had no hesitation though in asking for clothes and other materials unobtainable in India. Three other books continued the story of God's faithfulness over the years - but there were in fact many lean times and fervent prayers for daily bread. And for far more than that, as extensions to buildings became necessary. Great heart-searching and prayer for wisdom preceded every such decision. "The only expenditure, and all its outworkings, for which God can be held to be responsible, is that which He directs".

Houghton says ("Amy Carmichael of Dohnavur", page 143) that the pattern Amy was devising for the emerging Dohnavur Fellowship was "not given like the Tables of the Law, written in orderly fashion". But she did refer to it as "the Pattern shown in the Mount", and regarded it as from God, revealed in answer to prayer. More and more Indian, and some Western workers began to join the team. Amma set very high standards for those who came to work and live at Dohnavur. They could be asked to do any menial task, as she was prepared to, and often did. Above all, their lives, both individually and collectively, must be characterized by fervent love, humility and prayerfulness. Some failed these tests, and were asked to leave.

We must not conclude that Amy Carmichael was a a person with no time for fun. She was constantly finding enjoyable things for the children to do; nature study for one. She had an amazing gift for writing, exercised often when she was too exhausted for other work. We shall quote later from more serious pieces, but she could write nonsense rhymes for the girls' amusement, as well as songs of praise and worship, sometimes set by herself to simple Indian as well as Western tunes.

As a relief from the heat of the plains, a retreat centre was established among the forests on the nearby hills, and the family were taken there in turn, and on longer trips too.

In 1911 began a period of peculiar stress. Firstly, a child called Muttammal was rescued, only to be reclaimed, and later an application for custody was made by her relatives in court. "Amma" lost the case and had to pay costs; but in the apparent defeat, had a strong sense of God's presence. In her own account of what follows, she is very coy. It appears she had dropped an idea in the mind of a visitor from England. This woman took it on herself to escort Muttammal to another mission station, from where she was spirited away (quite willingly, of course) by stages to China! Several years later, she returned and married another convert, Arul Dasan, building supervisor.

Then there was the serious illness of Arulai, the death of her own loved Mother, and of a little favourite, Lulla, the need to "disappear" another child, Kohila, and the discovery that Ponnammal had cancer. She died in August 1915. Thomas Walker also died, just a week later. Criticism from other missionaries was often hard to bear. In this testing period, one poem sums up her feelings:

"O Thou Who art my quietness, my deep repose,
My rest from strife of tongues, my holy hill,

Fair is Thy pavilion, where I hold me still.
Back let them fall from me, my clamorous foes,
Confusions multiplied:
From crowding things of sense I flee, and in Thee hide
Until this storm be overpast,
Thy hand will hold me fast;
What though the tumult of the storm increase,
Grant to Thy servant strength, O Lord, and bless with peace".

By 1919, the storm was "overpast", for a while at least. The financial constraints of the First World War had ended, and her efforts to help the people of India had been recognized by the British government with a medal (she never collected it). She was encouraged by others to write more books on the growth of the work. A volunteer, Irene Streeter, became first representative of the Fellowship in Britain.

About this time, Amma also began the Sisters of the Common Life. Her purpose is not entirely clear. They were to be a group of women, mostly Indian to begin with, who consciously but not finally dedicated themselves to a single life, in order to serve unhindered. Amma was herself affected by her reading of the great mystics and encouraged extra dedication in the Sisters by reading these books aloud to them. Perhaps because of this new dedication, there was another touch of revival among the children in 1921.

There was however no thought of the work remaining only female. A few boys had been rescued from moral dangers, and Amma felt the great need for men to help. Over a long period, they were literally prayed in. After some less satisfactory applicants, two brothers, Murray and Godfrey Webb-Peploe, passed through Dohnavur on their way to missionary service in China. Amy felt immediately they were the right ones for the new departures God had laid on her heart; a hospital (Murray was a doctor), and a leader for the boys' work. Several years later, being obliged for different reasons to leave China, both applied to Dohnavur! They proved invaluable long-term servants of the Lord and the ministry there. But they did not arrive till 1926/27.

This was never to be "just another institution". Strenuous efforts were made to provide a real family atmosphere. The houseparents and other workers were referred to by Tamil words that mean "older sister" and "older brother". The children did some domestic jobs, but were encouraged to see this as part of what any child of a family would be expected to do. And Amy saw herself as Amma, Mother, of all, staff and children alike.

An exciting but ultimately tragic series of events surrounded Jambulingam, nicknamed Raj (King). He was an Indian Robin Hood, who stole from the rich and gave to the poor. Amma was led by God to meet him by his own decision (though also by her prayers). He decided to give himself up, once she promised to care for his children, and was jailed. Following a dream (a quite frequent occurrence, with Amma), she took a particular missionary, who had appeared in the dream, but needed great persuasion, to the prison to baptize the outlaw. Then he escaped, met her again, and again agreed to give himself up.

But before he could do so, he was betrayed to the police, and in trying to escape, shot at them and was then caught, tortured and finally despatched with a bullet to the head. Amma's book, "Raj, Brigand Chief" was an indictment of the Indian Police and prison system. Unfortunately, it made little difference, even under the British Raj. The British, always ultra-careful not to antagonize Hindus or Muslims, also did nothing about the practice of dedicating little girls to the gods. This was officially prohibited by the government of independent India, soon after 1947; but has not completely died out even yet.

It may have been the result of one intensely trying clash of personalities with a new worker (who later became a bishop, nearby), that Amy decided the work should no longer even in name be an outpost of the Church of England Zenana Mission. The independent, inter-denominational Dohnavur Fellowship was officially registered in 1927, just as the Webb-Peploe brothers were arriving. Their gifts, and those of others now on the staff, gradually persuaded Amma towards the idea of sharing the leadership, and deputing final authority. However, some years after this, and even after her first disabling accident, a new recruit could write: "She wouldn't proceed with any course of action until everyone had agreed; but who dare oppose her? We were awed - perhaps excessively so - by her wisdom and experience. She was a remarkable woman, alarming to a raw recruit, with a sort of aura about her". Others paid tribute to her humility and humour. But the demands and closedness of the place did cause a good number of workers to leave.

In 1931, Amma had the first serious accident, falling into a hole in the ground. This left her almost unable to walk. She spent the next twenty years hardly leaving the compound, and mostly in her own room. Often, she was racked with pain from neuralgia or neuritis. Later she suffered also from cystitis, high blood pressure, heart weakness, insomnia, and an eye condition. She described herself as "a toad under the harrow".

Nevertheless, she continued the overall supervision in various ways. Very gradually, changes were introduced at the instigation of others in the new leadership team. For instance the children, boys especially, were sent to outside schools for higher education. Games were added to the curriculum, for both sexes. She would earlier never have accepted either of these.

She wrote countless little notes of encouragement to both staff and children, with advice and thoughts from the Bible, as well as the assurance of her prayers. Anyone could arrange to see her personally, though by now she was unable to wander around the compound. And every day without fail, she wrote a thought on some verse of Scripture, which was intended as the basis of the daily worship. Nearly half of her more than thirty-five books were written after 1931. It is noticeable they were no longer biographies or narratives of God's provision, but more and more, devotional writings, of great depth.

Then there was her poetry. Frankly, it is of varied quality, but some of the pieces in her anthology, "Toward Jerusalem" are very fine by any standard. She loved the Authorised Version, with its "thee" and "thou", its "hast" and "wast", its "doeth" and "doth". Many allusions in her writings require an intimate knowledge of the Bible. In other words, the devotional ones are not "popular" reading for us today. Amazingly, she also found time to write several hundred songs, which were used in the Family's worship.

Although Dohnavur was in a back-water part of India, events in the wider world did impinge. The Fellowship subscribed to current events magazines, and Amy Carmichael had a good knowledge of political developments in Europe, leading up to the Second World War. But having German deaconesses working with many other nationalities at Dohnavur, she was careful not to discuss these things publicly. She often prayed for those affected by the War, especially the Blitz.

Even during the years when Dohnavur was a closed community, Amma came to the realisation that not all her girls and boys were turning out well. While she was ill, she would ask for some of the worst-behaved to be allocated to serve her; hoping to give them some status by this, and have more opportunities to show them love.

Arulai, her hoped-for successor, died in May 1939, another terrible blow as far as Indian leadership was concerned. For forty years she had been Amma's closest friend, first as an adopted daughter, then as companion in labour. Amma never seemed to feel any Indian man could be of equal dedication. Although she assured Godfrey that she would like him to take final authority, he never felt able to. After all, she could not leave the compound, and was revered by all. Dr. Murray Webb-Peploe returned to England for family reasons in 1947. Amma had another heavy fall in June 1948, and Godfrey Webb-Peploe himself died unexpectedly on February 19th, 1949.

But the work was firmly established. Other leaders such as Dr. May Powell could be relied upon, and more Indian leaders were emerging. In Amma's last two years of extreme weakness, she drew nearer and nearer to God, and her dying coma surely gave her an early sight of Him Whom her soul had always loved

so fervently. Her own poetic prayer of many years earlier was
abundantly fulfilled in her fragrant and fruitful life:

"*From prayer that asks that I may be*
Sheltered from winds that beat on Thee,
From fearing when I should aspire,
From faltering when I should climb higher,
From silken self, O Master, free
Thy soldier who would follow Thee.

From subtle love of softening things,
From easy choices, weakenings,
Not thus are spirits fortified,
Not this way went the Crucified,
From all that dims Thy Calvary,
O Lamb of God, deliver me.

Give me the love that leads the way,
The faith that nothing can dismay,
The hope no disappointments tire,
The passion that will burn like fire,
Let me not sink to be a clod:
Make me Thy fuel, Flame of God."

Allen Gardiner
1794 - 1851

❖

Allen Francis Gardiner was born at Basildon, Berkshire, the fifth son of convinced Christian parents. From his earliest years, he was fascinated by adventure and discovery. Horatio Nelson was his idol, and he intended from childhood to join the Royal Navy. His mother once going into the bedroom, discovered him sleeping on the wooden floor. When aroused, the little boy explained that he needed to harden his body for the rigours of the life he planned.

At 13 years old, he did indeed enter the Naval College at Portsmouth. In those days, only parental riches or influence could ensure an immediate commission, but he was taken under the wing of Lady Grey, a godly and motherly woman whose husband was Commissioner of the Dockyard. The lad's basic training occupied two years, then he went to sea as a cadet. Promoted to midshipman, he embarked on a Navy ship sent to stop American buccaneers attacking British merchant vessels in the Pacific. He had his first sight of South America, and near Valparaiso, his first experience of battle.

In that same year, his beloved mother died. Gradually, her godly influence and restraint faded from his mind, under the influence of companions and his exciting life-style. He began to be an active unbeliever, even arguing against the Christian faith. Yet from time to time, seeing ship-mates killed in accidents, his thoughts would become serious again. He even secretively bought a Bible, and began to read it in his more chastened moods.

Promoted to second lieutenant in 1814, he embarked on a long voyage to Cape Town, Ceylon, India, Malaysia and eventually China. Gradually, his thinking became more permanently turned to God. A spiritual crisis was precipitated by a letter from Lady Grey, describing the last few months of his mother's life, and her prayers for her son. Visiting a Buddhist temple in China, Gardiner began to ponder the emptiness of mere religion, versus the assurance of eternal life to be found in Jesus. He surrendered with all sincerity. His eternal choice was fixed.

Even before that, while in the Philippines, Gardiner had been confronted by the effects of the dominant Roman Catholicism. After visiting a tobacco factory, he wrote in his journal about the workers:

"The greater part of these people were Indians, and all professed Christianity. It is astonishing, how popular the Roman religion has always become among Pagans, and how easily it is grafted upon heathenism, to which it is in many respects too much allied. It is but to lay aside one set of rude and unmeaning images, and to adopt others, of a more attractive form, to barter stocks for saints, and turn devotion into a pleasing drama, and the Indian is conscious of no other difference."

By the time the ship passed New Zealand, crossed the Pacific, and reached Valparaiso, Chile, a civil war was going on in neighbouring Peru. The British (while still defending their own Empire!) were engaged in aiding the South American nationalists under General San Martin, as they fought for independence from Spain. There was time however for some shore leave, spent travelling to Santiago and through the mountainous North of Chile. Here, impressions of spiritual bondage and need were planted in the young naval officer, so recently born again.

The capture of Callao from the Spanish signalled the eventual freedom of both Peru and Chile in 1824. Gardiner's ship was this time not called upon to engage in war. On the way back to China, they called at Tahiti. There was an opportunity for Gardiner to see the results of work by the London Missionary Society. He was deeply impressed and challenged. The quick-tempered, adventure-loving lieutenant was already changing to a compassionate visionary.

When they reached Sydney, it became obvious that he was in poor health and needed a rest. He resigned his commission and took passage in a merchant vessel for Cape Town. By the time it reached there, he was physically restored, and his restless, energetic nature reasserted itself in a new direction - the needs of the Dark Continent of Africa. And even before reaching England again, he wrote to the L.M.S. about the question of starting a new outreach in South America. They were not convinced God was in this suggestion at the time. Neither was the Bishop of Gloucester, when Gardiner applied to him for ordination in the Church of England. God had hidden work still to do in this comparatively new recruit to the Kingdom, and was lovingly and wisely directing his steps.

He rejoined the Navy, attaining the rank of Commander, though he was never given a command of his own. He married Julia Reade, and five children were born to them over the next eight years; though two died in infancy. In 1834 Julia herself died, bringing to an untimely end what had truly been a marriage made in Heaven. Gardiner's journals reveal his deep love for her and gratitude to God, as well as a desire to submit without question or complaint to this sad parting.

It was a defining moment for Allen Gardiner. He determined to quit the Navy and devote his efforts to missionary work. This time without asking advice or permission from anyone, he set out for South Africa (since the door to South America seemed firmly closed). His plan was to go up-country to Zululand, and persuade Dingaan, a notorious chief, to become a Christian.

Phyllis Thompson ("An Unquenchable Flame", Hodder, 1983) writes with truth that the plan "seemed quixotic to the point of absurdity". The Zulus were a proud race of feared warriors and cattle thieves, and Britain had not yet subdued them. Restless Boer settlers, as Gardiner was to find, made another ingredient in the explosive mix.

But Gardiner was already a man deep in relationship with God and willingness to act by faith. Whatever we may think of this and later projects, it is noticeable that eventually they all resulted in spiritual fruit. In each place, sometimes years later, missionary activity began, on a long-term basis. God's way is not always the "sensible" or "prudent" way!

On the long passage from England to the Cape, Gardiner made the acquaintance of a Polish nobleman, travelling under the assumed name of Berken. He was en route to Australia to start a new life. Berken grew so attached to Gardiner he decided to accompany him in visiting the mission stations on the road to Port Natal. Just after they set off, skirmishes broke out between the land-hungry colonists and the Kafirs, as the black tribesmen were then called. The travellers were surreptitiously robbed of their oxen by members of one supposedly still friendly tribe. Gardiner immediately went unarmed to the chief and told him firmly the oxen must be returned. They were! Another time, he saved a dangerous situation by shaving a man!

Leaving Berken at Port Natal, Gardiner pressed on alone into Dingaan's territory. After finding the king and staying at his camp for a day or two, he felt uneasy, and departed secretly, making his way back through unfriendly country, with much resource and endurance. After a few months, he decided to try again, this time taking gifts with him. Dingaan made a grand gesture befitting one who thought grandly of himself. He bestowed a very large area of land on Gardiner, "for your own use". It was accepted, but on behalf of the King of England. Even better, he had Dingaan's assurance that any missionary sent would be protected and listened to.

When he reached Port Natal, it was to hear of the death by drowning of Berken, whom Gardiner admired for his "mental acquirements, his amiable character, and above all his genuine piety..." Gardiner marked out a parcel of Dingaan's "gift" for a Christian settlement he named Berea, and made plans for a larger town too. This time, he requested the Governor, Sir Benjamin D'Urban, if it could be named after him. And so Durban, today the capital city of Natal, was born.

It was time for a return to England, "mission accomplished" - or so it seemed. It was also God's time for Gardiner to meet and marry his second wife, Elizabeth Marsh, a clergyman's daughter less than half his age. It was a marriage that proved as happy as the first. Elizabeth was mature, affectionate, adaptable, and a good stepmother too. Apart from finding a house, he had to liaise with the Foreign Office about the Zulu situation, and also wrote a book about his travels in Natal. All, within less than a year. Then the family sailed again for Africa and the return to Berea. They were accompanied by a missionary, Francis Owen, sent by the C.M.S., and his family.

Tragically, the Gardiners' eldest daughter died on the way. Even this did not stop him from soon going on to Dingaan's camp to introduce the new missionary to the chief.

Just as things were developing nicely, the blow fell. The Dutch settlers had been joining with other tribes to attack the Zulus. A party of them who came to talk terms were treacherously murdered by Dingaan. Owen had to leave his post or probably, to forfeit his own life. Gardiner assumed (wrongly, it turned out later) the Zulu mission could not recommence for many years. Only Berea remained, as an outpost of the Gospel in the whole of Natal. It was time, he decided, to move on. But where? The opportunity presented itself to take a ship going to Rio De

Janeiro. He saw this as guidance, and the family embarked for another new life, arriving in June 1838.

John Marsh ("A Memoir of Allen F. Gardiner, Commander, R.N.", 1857), gives an account of the terrible effects of Spanish and Portuguese colonization in South America. He relates how the Jesuit missionaries had treated the Native Americans with kindness, and tried to educate them; but had also kept them in spiritual bondage to superstition and priestcraft. When their Order was proscribed by the Spanish king in 1767, "the Indians relapsed into barbarism". The removal of their protectors left the natives even more open to exploitation, And, despite the abolition of African slavery in Spain by 1830, it was still flourishing in South America. Gardiner was shocked by all of this, and saw the slaves (two-fifths of the population of Rio) as "a vast mission field" (Thompson). Had he not already determined to go to the Indian tribes of Chile, he might well have remained in Brazil to work amongst them. But the family had to journey on.

From Rio, all their belongings had to be transported by cart across the breadth of South America, to the other side of the High Andes. It was to be a journey of about 1000 miles in a Westerly direction, once they had reached Buenos Aires, in Argentina, by another sea voyage.

There were great dangers from Indian raiders on the pampas, who always killed their victims before robbing them. Right through the vast grasslands, they were plagued by fleas and lice. So it was a relief at last to reach Mendoza. Gardiner began to survey the possibilities for mission. He could immediately see that here was a great field for Bible distribution, and gave away all the Spanish Scriptures he had brought.

But it was onwards - and upwards, along the narrow ledges of the high Andes trails. On one occasion, Gardiner pulled his wife off her mule just as she was about to be knocked off it, by some protruding luggage on another pack animal's back. To fall over the edge would have meant certain death for human or beast.

They came safely to Santiago on the other side of the barrier, then Talca, Chilla, and Concepcion, where the family rested in their own accommodation. Gardiner, indefatigible and restless as ever, pressed on towards the South, and real Indian country. Meeting a friendly chief, he recorded in his journal: "Corbalan was informed of my desire to acquire his language in order that I might impart to his people the knowledge of the true God, as also of my wish to obtain his consent to bring my family, and reside in his immediate neighborhood. Such a proposal seemed altogether strange to his ears, still he made no objection, and after some further explanation, he seemed to enter cordially into it".

It was all to prove yet another blighted hope. Once Corbalan fully realised the white man intended to stay long-term, he forbad it completely, lest it should antagonise a stronger tribe nearby. On went Gardiner, to another area, another chief. He found, once again, that suspicions and rivalries engendered by Europeans, had preceded him. The second chief, Neggiman, at first expressed openness to teaching, providing the local Governor agreed. And that official might well have given permission, had his mind not been secretly poisoned against Protestant missionaries by a Friar Manuel (Gardiner was to discover this only later).

With a third tribe, it was prejudice against the Spanish, and the impossibility for Gardiner of distinguishing himself from them in their thinking. As Marsh summarizes the situation: "Thus thwarted in every effort, Allen Gardiner saw no hope remaining of getting at the heathen of South America. Fierce, exterminating warfare in some parts, led the Indian to look on every Christian as an enemy. Wherever peace reigned, Popery was dominant, and Protestant teaching was unwelcome".

Was it not time for a pause and careful thought about openings among the many nominal Christians in South America? "No", he said firmly, "I have devoted myself to God, to seek for openings among the heathen, and I cannot go back, or modify my vow". Marsh expresses it well: "He looked at the map of the world, as another man might look at that of Europe or England; and thought as little of going to the Antipodes, as a Londoner might, of going to York.... Any place seemed accessible to him, which he could approach by sea".

So off he dragged his family again, to seek out a tribe on the other side of the world! They sailed across the wide Pacific to Indonesia, under the impression that the Dutch colonial government, being Protestants, would put no obstacles in his way. A need to refit their ship meant they were just delivered from attack by Malay sea-pirates. Gardiner approached three officials responsible for New Guinea, who twisted and turned before finally refusing permission, on the ground that he was not Dutch. All the family got from this long trip, was fever.

Where, O where, could tribes be found, who were not already under harmful and powerful influences? Gardiner was frustrated at every turn; but his faith in God's ultimate purposes never wavered for an instant.

Returning to Valparaiso by sea, Gardiner made one final effort to find tribes, this time in the Gordillera mountains. He was followed around by the very same Friar Manuel who had turned the local government official against him earlier. Once more, he was refused permission to settle and begin work. Finally he concluded all doors were closed - except one. The very far South of Chile had been neglected even by the Catholics. Surely he could work unhindered there?

Slowly, while distributing Bibles and tracts with zeal every day, a plan came to his mind. Knowing the inhospitable climate and people of the far South, he determined to set up his headquarters on the Falkland Islands, and to use this as a jumping-off point for regular visits by boat to win the native tribes' confidence, while having a place of retreat, where his family could also reside in safety.

Not that the Falklands were exactly a desirable residence, being themselves cold, wet and windswept. It was, for the family, "Farewell to Chili". Under that title, here is a sample of Gardiner's poetry, which shows considerable ability; and also his deep, dependent and trusting relationship with God, and constant burden for lost souls:

> *"The Indian defies thee, white man, though thy slave,*
> *He grasps his long lance his fair border to save:*
> *But his valour is vain (though as free as the air)*
> *When you rivet on him the same chains that you wear,*
> *And exclude the true light, which alike you might share.*
>
> *Oh, speed on the morn, Lord, thy promise fulfil,*
> *Pierce the gloom with thy brightness - thy Spirit instil:*
> *Even now cause some beams of the forthcoming day*
> *On Andes' cold turrets to flicker and play,*
> *Till the sun in his strength bids the shadows decay".*

(Santiago, October 23, 1841)

The Indians of Patagonia were notorious for killing mariners wrecked on their shores. Charles Darwin, who had recently made his famous voyage around Cape Horn in the "Beagle", to do his scientific observations on the Galapagos Islands, had firm opinions on them. He declared they could never be civilised. Some years later, being informed of the work of the Gospel there, he admitted his mistake, and gave a subscription to the South American Missionary Society. The Gospel has transformed many groups thought unchangeable! But before Patagonia could be effectively reached, much cross-bearing was called for.

Finding accommodation again for his family, Gardiner was told of a Creole man, by the name of San Leon, who was living among the tribes, where he was regarded as a very great medicine-man, because he had shot one who tried to put a curse on him, and lived to tell the tale! In a somewhat optimistic way, Gardiner thought this man might be able to help him gain the confidence of the Patagonian Indians. He began to look for a vessel to take him to the mainland. It was the height of the whaling season, and while fishing-boat captains expressed their general willingness to take him across and back, they flatly refused to interrupt their short profitable season at any price.

Gardiner, brooking no delay, found a small schooner that was barely seaworthy and had been recaulked by its owner (to take advantage of the missionary's generous terms). It struggled across to the Straits of Magellan, and eventually Indians were sighted and approached with small gifts. This removed their unwelcoming scowls, but only momentarily. It was clear they wanted no other communication. They made unmistakable signs that the white men should depart forthwith. At a second location, the famous San Leon was met. He told them, in Spanish, that some earlier American missionaries had had to depart, because the Indians stole all their possessions.

More of the tribe returning the next day gave the visitors the opportunity to observe ther social organisation, which was simple but efficient. While they talked, news came that a disagreement had arisen between the schooner's crew and some natives from Tierra Del Fuego, the large island which is the continent's fractured Southern end. The crew departed, taking San Leon to Port Famine, and leaving Gardiner and the ship's owner, a Mr. Johnson, to negotiate with the natives by sign language only. The people here were just curious and light-fingered, not threatening.

After the "Montgomery" returned, another tribe arrived, under a chief called Wissale. With them was a Negro, named Isaac, who claimed to have deserted from a whaler, and seemed to be a much better interpreter than Leon, since he spoke English fluently. Again, presents were given, and Wissale expressed great openness to the idea of a missionary residing with them to teach the Gospel. The prospects sounded good, and Gardiner began to think of purchasing a plot for a house, and bringing over his family.

Back to the Falklands he went, and looked for passage on some trading vessel large enough to convey them in safety. A whole six months passed with no success. During this time, Gardiner sent a report to the C.M.S., and asked their help in finding a man to continue what he hoped was a long-term opening among this apparently friendly tribe. Back came a letter with the discouraging news that C.M.S. was passing through a financial crisis, which forbad them recruiting new missionaries. Allen Gardiner decided to go to England. The family sailed in October 1842, on the way meeting a whaler whose crew conveyed the welcome news that San Leon had made good his promise to protect the hut and belongings Gardiner had left behind.

The Gardiner children now needed to continue their education on a more formal basis. The family no longer travelled with him. Disappointed by C.M.S, he next applied to the Wesleyan and London Missionary Societies, with equal lack of success. Marsh explains it like this:

"There was little response to this appeal; for when the disasters, which had overtaken the Zulu mission, were recalled to mind, there were few, whose warm enthusiasm in the cause did not cool. It is a long time before our countrymen can be persuaded of the importance of anything, which does not form a part of that inheritance of prejudices, which they have received from their fathers. There seemed to be an infatuation on the subject of South America. While efforts to spread Christianity in other parts of the world were carried on with vigour, all animation died, when South America was but hinted at. All, with one consent, began to make excuse. Eyes filled with dreamy somnolency at the prospect, and collective voices seemed to say with a soft murmur, 'It is the natural inheritance of pope and pagan: let it alone'".

The indomitable Gardiner was not to be stopped. He remembered how eagerly the Scriptures at least had been received in Chile, and proceeded there yet again, attempting in part to show his critics how the Gospel door could be opened in Latin America.

"Hesitation was a quality which he did not understand. With a frame of iron, and nerves which never flinched from fatigue or danger, he broke with dauntless vehemence through every difficulty which beset his path. He was always ready to meet the attacks of friends or foes, listening and replying to opposing arguments, but never turned from the object before him. He never entered on a new enterprise without very much and earnest prayer for divine guidance. When visiting any of his friends, he generally found some straight path in the garden, which he paced like a quarter-deck, for hours each day, in the deepest study of God's holy Word. Whatever might be the breakfast hour, he was always up an hour before, for prayer and the study of the Bible. Such a man was not likely to be turned from his purpose".

Arriving off the Eastern coast, Gardiner was again confronted by a semi-war, this time between Argentina and Uruguay, which delayed his arrival in Montevideo, capital of the latter country. Once able to land, he travelled to Santa Fe and Cordoba distributing tracts, but reserving his stock of Bibles and other books for Santiago. A Dr. Gordon and a local, Don Jose Maria Lopez. arranged a reception, at which many of the upper class people of the city bought books in large numbers.

Next, Gardiner journeyed to Tucuman Province, nursing a very inflamed throat. Two hundred Testaments were accepted for resale by a bookseller, and even Catholic padres accepted them as gifts. One then announced from his pulpit that this version was heretical. It took all Gardiner's persuasion to convince the police otherwise. Later, the priest revised his opinion.

Gardiner was elated and grateful to God. "He had proved, that no real power of prohibition remained to the priests". Arming himself with two pistols, he passed safely through the areas infested by bandits, arrived at Buenos Aires, Montevideo and eventually, after seven months absence, in England. He had been further encouraged by a promise of financial support from English-speaking congregations in four South American cities, for a new mission to Patagonia.

The situation with established British missionary societies had not substantially changed in his absence. Having met several able, interested men while living in Brighton, who could act as committee, Gardiner was led to begin a new one; the Patagonian Missionary Society. The surprising amount of money subscribed in a short time, encouraged the committee to agree in sending a young school-teacher, John Hunt, to Patagonia. Allen Gardiner accompanied Hunt, expecting only to settle him in comfortably.

Arriving on the inhospitable shore again, with enough supplies for several months, and three huts for shelter, they were surprised when a Chilean, who had deserted from his country's new settlement at Port Famine, staggered up to their door, exhausted. Recovered from his ordeal, he gave the unwelcome news that Chile was now trying to pacify the tribes so as to establish its own rule in the far South, against the Argentinian counter-claims. This was being accomplished by a combination of food distribution, and religious teaching; Catholic, of course. San Leon was working for them, and had attracted around himself many of Wissale's tribe.

Next, the much reduced in status chief himself appeared, seemingly just as glad as before to see the Englishmen. It soon became clear, however, that there was a difference of opinion between them. Marsh says that whereas Gardiner wanted to husband his resources for a long stay, Wissale felt that all available food should be consumed (by his own family and tribe, mainly), and that the question of what to do when it ran out was a churlish, insulting one to ask! He was also greatly under the influence of another Spaniard called Cruz, who appeared occasionally, and whose influence was wholly against the missionaries. At last, the demands and then threats of the chief became just too much, and Gardiner and Hunt (who later took ordination, and then became a C.M.S. missionary elsewhere), had to return yet again to Britain, minus all their supplies, and with absolutely no progress to report.

Supporters were devastated. The Committee refused to send another expedition meantime. Gardiner the unquenchable decided on another "final final" trip to Bolivia, in search yet again of an opening. He would pay his own expenses. Montevideo was reached on September 22nd, 1845. This time Gardiner was accompanied by a young Spanish Protestant, Federico Gonzales, who had been accepted by the Society in Gardiner and Hunt's absence - for Patagonia!

The on-off wars between Argentina, Paraguay, and now Brazil, hindered a land crossing to the west. Instead, they had to re-embark for Valparaiso around Cape Horn, wasting four months. In Montevideo, Gardiner had become friendly with a merchant named LaFone, who is to feature sadly, later in our story.

It was decided to proceed onwards to Coliga in Bolivia by boat. Then through the dusty Atacama Desert they went, to Calama, and finally Cobija. Remarkably, since the Jesuits had departed, there was "Now not a single mission in the Chaco, and the whole country is before us. Beyond the Pilcomayo...the Indians are as much independent of Bolivia as the natives of China are". And, "This day, by the blessing of God, we have finished our long and tedious journey, by a road, or rather track, so bad, that probably few are worse in any part of the world. For the last two days, it has led us through a thick forest, and we are half-devoured by large flies and mosquitoes. But the Lord has graciously protected us, and brought us here in health, blessed be His holy name". Gonzales, a much younger man, was left very ill! by these journeys. Gardiner continued to wander between tribes for weeks, talking to chiefs. His own fevers made this a marathon indeed. Finally, cholera struck him down. The iron man was left weak and helpless.

At this low point, enter the Bolivian Provincial Governor, with medical help, and good advice too. Why not present an official petition directly to the President, Senor Balinian? He was sympathetic to Protestants and certainly not ruled by priests! On a more personal level, Gardiner was now able to resume letters to and from his family and others. Despite a pessimistic prediction by the British Consul, the President did indeed grant permission, at least for a mission station from which tribes across the Northern and Western borders of Bolivia might be reached. Gonzales began to learn the language of the Quechuas. Gardiner returned to England. Another Spanish missionary was employed and sent. The government of Bolivia changed. Priests reasserted their authority over the new one. The door slammed shut on Gardiner's hopes, yet another time.

Phyllis Thompson heads her seventh chapter with the title of her biography; "Unquenchable Flame" - a fitting description of Allen Gardiner. His second book, "A Voice from South America", now appeared. It was an eye-opener, and a challenge. Thompson reflects that if his first attempt at Patagonia had been a "success", the Church would have had no such general survey.

Allen Gardiner's thoughts now began to turn once more towards Patagonia - or to be more precise, Tierra del Fuego. This "Land of Fire" was detached from the Southern end of the continent, and consisted of several large islands, linked by dangerous but navigable channels. The people were somewhat different from other Patagonians, and even more uncivilized.

The weather was colder, the winds wilder. In fact, Tierra del Fuego had only one thing in its favour. No country owned it!

Some thirty years earlier, a Captain Fitzroy of the Royal Navy had landed there from his survey vessel, and had taken four young natives back to England for education. Later they were returned to their native place, and might be traceable, to act as interpreters for new arrivals. Also, the Fuegians seemed to have a remarkable aptitude for imitating the language and gestures of Europeans, in mockery. This, it was hoped, meant they could learn English easily!

After trying unsuccessfully to raise enough funds for a permanent work, Gardiner decided to go on a trip to reconnoitre and bring back hard information on possibilities. In January 1848, the "Clymene", en route for Peru, took on board five men and their equipment, including a "decked boat", and supplies for a six months stay.

Arriving amid the maze of the Magellan Straits, the small boat was launched and struggled ashore in a high wind. A suitable place was found as base, and named "Banner Cove". The wind increasing to a tempest, they had to walk across the island and board the ship in a more sheltered place. Their activities had attracted an increasing number of curious tribepeople. and when the party began to unload supplies, it became increasingly obvious the natives were intent on pilfering everything. Very reluctantly, Gardiner concluded a land base was impossible to maintain. They would just have to operate from offshore.

"I should recommend a ketch or brigantine, of about 120 tons, with a master and seven hands. Provisions for twelve months should be taken out; but three fourths should be deposited at the Falklands, where, as opportunities occurred, supplies should afterwards be forwarded from England, and placed in charge of an agent appointed for the purpose".

On his way back from Peru, Gardiner had further opportunity to see that South America was open at least to distribution of the Scriptures. Home early in August 1848, he spent the next one and a half years trying to get support for buying a ship of the kind he had described. Still no larger society was willing to adopt the work or provide funds for it. A Committee was re-formed, with Rev. Pakenham Despard of Bristol as Secretary. With still limited income, Gardiner made what, with the wonderful gift of hindsight, we can see was his first fatal mistake. For the original large vessel, he substituted two small vessels of only twenty-eight feet length.

He made no mistakes in the men who were to accompany him. Joseph Erwin had gone as carpenter on the exploratory trip, though apparently not a born-again Christian. He did have enormous love and respect for his leader: "Being with Captain Gardiner was like a heaven upon earth, he was such a man of prayer". Two "catechists" were to be stationed long-term; Richard Williams, medical doctor from the Potteries who had given up a flourishing practice, and John Maidment, who had worked for the Y.M.C.A. in London. Then there were three "frank, brotherly Cornish fishermen, Pearce, Badcock and Bryant".

Receiving a typically up-beat letter from Gardiner, the Committee sent out supplies; but this is where the second ingredient of tragedy was added. Unable to find a vessel to convey them directly, they decided to ship the stores to the

Falklands, confident (from Gardiner's statements) that boats plied regularly from there to Tierra del Fuego.

Meanwhile, the intrepid missionaries were finding their two vessels inadequate. First, both dinghies were lost in high seas. Then the "Pioneer" was grounded by the tide. Threatening natives appeared and were disarmed by prayer (temporarily at least). The "Pioneer" was again grounded, this time by a fierce storm, and its timbers stoven in on rocks. Its crew had to find shelter in a cave at Spaniard Harbour. It was only early Autumn (February); even worse weather was to come.

The party settled down to wait for relief, expecting that their supplies would last several weeks at least. True, it had been a blow to find that all the gunpowder had been left behind in the Falklands. There was little possibility of shooting wild fowl to supplement their diet of ships biscuit. Even fish were mysteriously few in the sea.

Within a few days, sickness commenced. First, Mr. Williams took scurvy. Here, he had opportunity to find that Gardiner, who had first struck him as "unjust, cold and censorious", was a sympathetic and loving person underneath the shell of naval disciplinarian. Gardiner in his turn discerned that the more emotional doctor was a real and sacrificial Christian. Harmony prevailed amongst them, despite the increasing hunger and other difficulties. Damp clothes brought Williams low again. Then Badcock, one of the Cornishmen, sickened and died very quickly.

Why had relief not come? A terrible series of events meant that the ship-captain charged with conveying supplies from the Falklands sailed before his instructions arrived. Then they were mistakenly filed away for months. Even Samuel LaFone from Montevideo, who had independently arranged to send some by ship, was frustrated three times over by various accidents, including a shipwreck.

On the beach and in the cave, starvation was weakening all. The final weeks of the men's lives were however distinguished by marvellous trust and hope. Gardiner's journal and poems are heart-rending and challenging. His attitude was all praise, submission and petition for the Kingdom's success:

"Grant O Lord, that we may be instrumental in commencing this great and blessed work; but shouldest Thou see fit in Thy providence to hedge up our way, and that we should even languish and die here, I beseech Thee to raise up others, and to send forth labourers into this harvest. Let it be seen, for the manifestation of Thy glory and grace, that nothing is too hard for Thee...

June 28, Saturday, my birthday".

He died near the upturned boat in September 1851. His and others' bodies were found by Captain Morshead of H.M.S. "Dido" four months later. Gardiner's journals and last report were water-damaged but readable.

And from that desolate shore, a work did indeed begin. Initial recriminations in Britain gave way to a determination not to allow the brave martyrs to die in vain. The South American Missionary Society, as it became, had as one of its first candidates, Gardiner's own son. He was to extend the Mission into Chile, as his father had hoped. The tribes of Cape Horn were reached too, and many others in Paraguay and up into the Northern Chaco. The buried seeds brought forth abundant fruit.

Afterthoughts

---------------------------------- ❖ ----------------------------------

These short lifestories are not fully representative of the ongoing missionary enterprise, in that they include only two women. At least since Edwardian times, women, and particularly single women, have made a greater and greater contribution to the cause of missions. This may reflect the natural self-giving which seems to be more often a female charcteristic, than a male one. It also reflects badly on men's present willingness to take on the harder and less obviously rewarding or status giving jobs in overseas mission. May these missionary men's lives be a challenge especially to today's Christian young men.

Secondly the book, depicting as it does past conditions, does not properly reflect a seachange that is coming about in overseas mission. More and more workers are having to go as "tent-makers". This convenient piece of Biblical shorthand means, not going as upfront missionaries, but employing professional skills to enter otherwise closed countries and serve their peoples, taking whatever opportunities may arise, to witness by word. Patrick Johnstone, in "Operation World" reports, "There are about 60 nations in the world where this is the major way for gaining entry into a country, and in 33 of these it is the only way". In some ways, an even more demanding calling than conventional missionary work.

Finally, some acknowledgements by the author. I have been writing these short biographies in spare time over many years. I am indebted to Margot Williams for typing the earlier ones, to Monica Gulley, Northumbria Bible College and the South American Missionary Society for access to printed sources. And to SIM, my own society, for not questioning extra time spent in preparing the material for publication! Also, for the source material on Harry Merriweather. The research and writing has been a great challenge to me. May it be so to others who read this book.